Glory to Glory

Glory to Glory

A Book about Change

SETH SOKOLOFF

Foreword by Richard Senkungu

RESOURCE *Publications* · Eugene, Oregon

GLORY TO GLORY
A Book about Change

Resource Publications
An Imprint of Wipf and Stock Publishers
199 W. 8th Ave., Suite 3
Eugene, OR 97401

www.wipfandstock.com

PAPERBACK ISBN: 978-1-5326-7352-8
HARDCOVER ISBN: 978-1-5326-7353-5
EBOOK ISBN: 978-1-5326-7354-2

Manufactured in the U.S.A.   APRIL 30, 2019

This book is dedicated to my partner in change, my wife, Diana. She seemingly, so effortlessly, walks side by side with me through all that life can throw at us.

Contents

Foreword

I FELT A GREAT honor when Seth asked me to write a foreword for this book on change. Over the last close to ten years, I have seen change happen to Seth while he served in and at Life Church here in Kampala, Uganda (and to myself since we are like peers) and how he has responded rightly at every opportunity of change.

Therefore, in many ways, I see Seth relaying out the story of his life (thus far) while giving us snippets of change. I have always wanted him to document some of the testimonies, especially in his earlier years and how God miraculously encountered him, healed him, and put him on a journey of purpose and fruitfulness that we have all been able to partake of.

We all know that healthy things grow, and growth is the fruit of change (metamorphosis). Change is, therefore, an opportunity that God has given us to move from one place of, especially infancy, and then move onto maturity. This book gives us an opportunity to see change in a new way rather than abhor it. Yes, there are moments when we are seemingly victims of unnecessary change; for example, in civil wars, the death of a loved one, closed doors in our lives, natural calamities, etc. In such moments, I am comforted from the thought that God, who is the creator of the entire universe, is still in charge of every circumstance. This book reminds us that God is timeless and is the author of all change. He is from before time and therefore, nothing catches Him by surprise.

Through this book, we will be encouraged to continuously look to God, the author and finisher of our life.

The stories told in this book are not fiction; Seth tells the journey of his life and how change has happened to him and caused a necessary growth in his life. Constantly as we read, we will be thrown into a new thought of seeking to see God in our moments of "change." Not only that, but also how He has all of it working together for our good if we seek to love Him and walk in His purpose for our lives.

> And we know that in all things, God works for the good
> of those who love him, who have been called according
> to His purpose
> (Romans 8:28, NIV)

RICHARD SENKUNGU
Lead Pastor, Life Church Uganda

Preface

IF THERE IS ONE thing that I have had to learn to deal with, it is change. By the time I was 21 years old, I had moved twelve times across states, continents, and countries. Change was never a "what if" for me, but a guaranteed part of life. I believe this to be true for everyone. Change is a promised reality of life. Some may experience more changes than others, but everyone will experience ample amounts of change in their life. It truly is one of the only things that I can say is guaranteed.

I watched change affect many parts of my life both positively and negatively. A constant for me was my ability to be unprepared every time change found me. Changing friends, schools, locations, and everything in-between is something that as young people, we have to learn to be prepared for. Change can be scary and extremely trying at times, but I have learned that as a promised part of life, it is something that can be used to bring us closer to the things God has for us. If we are not careful, it can also be used to take us further away. Change has the unique ability to take even the strongest, and most-put-together person, and spin them around so fast that they don't even know which way is up.

Change is not a joking subject.

I have taken the last season and tried to look through the past seasons of change that I have walked through. Through journals, thoughts, and a few tears, I have tried to dissect change and be extremely honest about it. I have not handled change correctly many times, but through learning, I believe I have become better at it. I don't know where you find yourself today reading this book. You may consider yourself an expert at change, a novice, or like me, simply someone who is learning along the way. No matter where you are, I know two things for sure: God wants to change your view of change, and you can either ignore this very real part of life or face it head-on.

Change can help us become all that God wants us to be, or it can chew us up, and spit us out, looking worse than it found us. I wasn't prepared for many of the changes when they found me initially. Some I had control over, and others happened before I was even born. My prayer is that this book would find you early enough so that you can be open and honest about all things called change.

Are you ready for change?

Ready or not, it is coming—in small forms and large areas. Let's change our view of change so that we truly can be changed from glory to glory, no matter what!

Part I

Introduction to Change

I

Change Guaranteed

EVERYONE WATCHED WITH EAGER expectation as I turned over the card that I had pulled out of the deck. I had the entire group's attention fixed on this single moment in time. I watched their faces as I showed them the card that I thought they had chosen just a few moments earlier . . .

I certainly wouldn't call myself a magician, but I know a few card tricks that I enjoy showing people. My wife thinks they're cheesy, but I think they're awesome! Who doesn't enjoy causing people to second guess what they have just seen? Responses vary from people rolling their eyes to people thinking I'm practicing witchcraft (Don't worry; I'm not). The whole point of magic tricks is to trick people into thinking that change happened magically instead of logically. It goes against "what should have happened," and makes us believe that something else caused the change. What nature has promised us as certain, the right trick can convince us otherwise. Cards don't appear out of nowhere, so how did this one come out of my jacket? We can find ourselves questioning what we know to be certain, simply by the way a change took place. Change is extremely powerful.

There have been many times that I missed a step in a card trick, and it didn't go right. I will find myself at the very end of the trick, with all eyes wide open expecting the "trick," only to drop the cards, or realize that I have done a step wrong. I have now lost the confidence of all onlookers, and have effectively embarrassed myself. The change that should have taken place, either took place at the wrong time or didn't take place at all. Not only is the change powerful, but also when, and how, it takes place. Hopefully, if you ever try your hand at magic tricks, you'll find yourself to be a better magician than I am.

Life can, sometimes, feel like it has "tricked" us. Some things suddenly don't turn out the way we expected them to. We are faced with the consequences and have to decide what to do next. A "guaranteed" thing like your parents staying together or the health of a loved one, can almost instantly change and no longer seem so certain, and safe, as they once did. These life-altering changes very often do not make sense in the moment that they occur.

> "I was supposed to move from my home for college, and not in the middle of high school. Certainly not because my mom lost her job!"

> "I thought my job would be permanent, and that my position was secure. How can it simply be over?"

> "I have always done things this way with the same result. Why are they not working this time?"

According to our understanding of life up to this point, these changes should not have happened. At the very least, we would have had a little more warning before they did. Right? We don't always get the opportunity to decide how things will happen. We are often thrown into the mix of something that we were not ready for, and like witnessing a well-performed magic trick, we find ourselves questioning everything that we were certain of just before this moment.

While I was growing up, I experienced many changes that I did not expect. Many things that I felt were unchangeable, suddenly changed without notice. Things that I considered permanent seemed to change as easily as the second hand on a clock. Ninety-nine percent of the time, the change caught me off guard. I simply was not ready for the change to take place, and when it suddenly did, I found myself questioning everything. I had not yet changed my view of change. I allowed the change that took place around me to completely rattle me internally, and this negative change inside of me, led to me making wrong changes around me. While we cannot decide when change happens, we can decide how we allow it to change us.

Change can completely alter our understanding of dreams, the future, and even who we are. It can, in a moment, dismantle things that have taken a lifetime to build. Change can make the strongest feel weak, and the most secure feel insecure. These shifts can throw out certainties and make what's temporary become permanent. Change can cause you to question things that you already had the answer to, and force you to make decisions that you thought you would never have to make.

Change will change you.

Change . . . It can take you from glory to glory, or it can take you to places you never wanted to go. The question is, which will it be for you?

Change is a guaranteed part of life. From the time you start high school until you get married, you face the most concentrated amount of change than in any other season of your life. Body changes, emotional changes, location changes, friend changes, financial changes, future changes, roles in relationships change, responsibility changes, and just about everything else. The way things change . . . changes. We are often not ready for most of these and often react to the change, instead of being prepared for it, and learning how to change with it.

Throughout this book, I pray that you will change your view of change, and become someone who will be able to stand on the other side of change, closer to what God wants and not further away. I desire that God will help each one of us view circumstances, whether we are in control of them or not, with such faith in Him, that we glory in change because we are walking hand-in-hand with the Creator of the World.

Grapes

We define just about everything as "healthy" based on how it changes. Could you imagine if a baby simply didn't grow or change? If while we celebrated this baby's 10th birthday it looked exactly the same as the day it was born, we would all agree that something was wrong because the baby hadn't changed. If a plant doesn't grow and change, we either blame the plant for being unhealthy or the gardener for failing at their job. Imagine the sun never setting and the day never changing to night. We would say that something is out of the ordinary because of the lack of change. Change is a part of everything. Our world is based on change, but we are so often thrown off base when it comes our way.

My grandfather has been a grape farmer in Northern California for all his life. He started farming at an incredibly young age. He can read seasons, weather patterns, and make a decision based on the color of a leaf better than anyone. He can look at the sky at 7:00 am and tell you what the weather will be like at 2:00 pm. He can smell soil and tell you what is in it, and what is not. He is like a master chef . . . of plants. He has more than just a green thumb; he has a green arm. If you didn't know better, you would think he was the Hulk, because of his overwhelming greenness. Okay, maybe that's an exaggeration, but you get the picture.

He, like most farmers, has learned to study how plants change. Farming isn't always very profitable, so to help compensate lean harvests, he also started a nursery in his front yard. Every summer, for the early part of my life, I would spend time on this farm in Northern California. I learned to do many things during these summers. I learned how to both receive and prevent sunburns, pick weeds, crash and fix all sorts of vehicles, weld, how to wake up way too early, and how to make plants grow.

Maybe it was because I always went at the same time of year for about the same amount of time, but it seemed as if this place never changed. It was always hot and dry. The vineyards were always green and stretched in every direction as far as the eye could see. My grandfather was always old with a massive white beard, and walked with a limp (from literally getting hit by a train); for as long as I could remember, this never changed. The air always smelled like dust, and there was rarely a cloud in the sky. Nothing outwardly seemed to change. I idolized this farm and was convinced that surely one day, I would also become a farmer. Ironically, it was in this seemingly unchanging place that I learned some of my most important lessons about change.

One of the most important things in farming is monitoring the growth and the change of the factors that make grapes grow (weather, water, soil, insects, etc.). A good farmer can solve problems that keep growth from happening and quickly change their approach if it isn't working. If the crop is not growing and maturing as it should, there is a problem. You then attempt to fix the problem and only if the plant begins to grow again can you confirm that the "fix" worked. Sometimes, the "fix" is as simple as watering more, and other times, the problem is actually more complex like an infestation of a certain type of bug. Once in a while, the change would be as instant as an hour or day, if the solution worked and other times, it took a week or more, to see a difference. There were both good and bad changes, but everything revolved around change. You are considered a good farmer if you make the right adjustments in response to the different changes that occur.

My grandfather grew grapes, and one of the most crucial stages in growing this type of crop is the "ripening" stage. You spend the whole year preparing for this limited window of time when the grapes ripen and "change" to the point you want them to. Different markets for the crop need the grapes at different stages in this ripening process. You can sell them to grocery stores for eating, sell them to a factory for making juice concentrate or wine, or lay them on tray papers and make raisins with the power of the sun. Each of these potential markets calls for a different handling and sugar level in the grapes.

On his farm, my grandfather had this fancy device that looked like a miniature telescope. I don't know the proper name for it, but he called it the "sugar meter." It did just that; it showed you how much sugar was present in the grapes at that particular moment. You squeeze out some grape juice onto the sugar meter and then hold it up to the sun, and it somehow shows you the sugar level. One big issue would be if the grapes were not ripening fast enough. If they were not changing according to what was normal, it would prove that there was a problem. When it comes to farming, change is celebrated and worked towards constantly.

What about in life?

One of the most guaranteed things in life is often avoided and not prepared for. If change is guaranteed and necessary for everything else in the world, why is it so hard to accept, and what do we do with it when it comes?

My prayer through this book is that God will help open our eyes and allow us to be honest about change. That we will through the next chapters see that even unexpected change can be used by God to move us closer to all that He has for us. I have experienced a lot of changes up to this point in my life, and I believe God can help you, just as He has helped me in navigating all of life's changes. He can also help you learn from the past to change the outcome of the future.

Throughout this book, I am going to be as vulnerable as possible, knowing that we truly overcome the enemy by the blood of the Lamb and the word of our testimony! (Revelations 12:11)

I have handled some of the changes in my life well, and others not so well. Some of the changes I was expecting and even initiated, and some were completely unexpected, and I tried to run from them. Even today, I don't understand all of them, but I do know that God is involved in *all* aspects of change and life.

Change can truly be used to take us from glory to glory if we allow it to. God desires to continually ensure that we look more and more like His Son, Jesus, and that takes constant change. If I were to stop growing in my relationship with God, I would actually be moving backward. There is no middle ground. We are either moving closer to Him or further away. We are either changing to look more like Him or less like Him. We all have the potential to grow in our understanding of change, and allow God to assist in giving us the tools needed to handle change correctly.

Are you open to change your view of change?

Questions for change

1. What is your first thought when you hear the word change? (Good or bad?)

2. What is the most difficult change you've gone through?

3. Do you think God can truly be involved in every change we experience? (What about bad changes?)

2

The Greatest Change

THE GREATEST "CHANGE" IN human history occurred when Jesus Christ set foot on earth.

The greatest change takes place in our history when Jesus Christ sets foot in our heart!

God is the author of change. (We will spend a majority of chapter 4 looking at what this means). His coming in human flesh completely altered history for the rest of eternity. There has never been, and never will be, a bigger shift in humanity than the day that Jesus set foot on earth. His coming, living a sinless life, dying on the cross, resurrecting on the third day, and ascending to heaven, has permanently changed the universe. He gave an answer to the human condition that many do not even know is being asked in the human heart. The world, often unaware of their need, is crying out for an answer for the lack that is inside of them. It is this change that answers every question that the human heart can ask!

This change, occurring over 2,000 years ago, set the stage for the largest change that you and I can encounter—meeting Jesus Christ for ourselves. I am not talking about subscribing to a certain religion or sect of Christianity, but truly beginning a relationship with the Savior of the World—coming to a place where you can talk to God, and He genuinely talks back to you. A living, breathing, and growing relationship. Relationship with God is a foreign concept to some, and to many, something that seems impossible. It could be from past experiences or broken natural relationships, but the thought of a healthy relationship with God the Father may seem unachievable. It is this relationship and encounter that will completely alter your past, present, and future. It is through this change that other changes can be handled and viewed correctly.

The meeting that forever changed me

I remember the first time I met Jesus. I had heard about Him to some extent, but I don't know that I could have told you my full opinion of what I thought of Him. There were, at least, a few things about Him that I had heard about. He had something to do with Christmas, and some people had a picture of Him on necklaces. While drinking eggnog and opening presents, I may have even thanked Him for being born so that I could selfishly indulge in the season. Probably because of T.V., a picture of a baby faced, "Fabio-esque," long-haired dude wearing a dress, picture was in my mind when His name was mentioned. Up to the moment that Jesus met me, I was very far from a correct understanding of the person of Jesus with plenty of wrong ideas about Him.

Church was not a normal part of life in my home while growing up. I had a desire for attention and the acceptance of others, and I sought them in the wrong ways. My relationship with my Mom felt strained from different circumstances, and it seemed to be continually getting worse. I had never met my father and was disconnected from other extended family. My wife hears different stories from this season from other people and simply can't believe that it was the same person she knows today. What is funny, is that I considered myself a pretty good person. Sure, I ding-dong ditch people's houses, made fun of people less fortunate than me, and had been in jail, but I was a "good person" compared to others.

In all honesty, I was quite simply the opposite of what you would think of a follower of Jesus looks like.

A rather large change was the precursor to me meeting Jesus. After my freshman year of high school, my Mom and I moved states to distance ourselves from an unsafe relationship. I quickly found and fell in love with downhill mountain biking when we moved to Oregon from California. This sport became an identity for me and helped me medicate myself with the drug of adrenaline. The hurt that I felt inside did not hurt as much when I was hurling myself down steep hills and off jumps. Crashing hurt, but it was a different kind of hurt, and one that I could deal with. One of the first days of summer break when I was 16 years old, I was at my friend's house getting ready to go for a ride. Before loading our bikes in his truck, we decided to ride around the neighborhood a bit. One of the houses close to my friend's house had a driveway that was quite steep going up to the house. Off the side of the driveway was a drop to grass with a sidewalk running through it. It looked like the perfect place to jump off for fun.

I decided that I would go first and then my friend would follow. I rode to the edge of the driveway, and instead of jumping off the side, I fell off the side. I swan-dived directly onto my head. Of course, I found the only piece of sidewalk around and not the grass. The moments that followed would completely alter my life forever.

Face planting onto concrete is never a recommended activity. I split my helmet right down the middle, along with my scalp, and skull. It was as if you dropped a watermelon on the ground by accident. My friend said I kept screaming the word, "jelly." The more I think about it, I was probably trying to say his name, Jeremy, or I just wanted a PB&J. We will never know. After some moments of shock, he went and called 911. My memory is obviously limited due to my massive head injury, but what I do remember completely changed me.

While lying on the ground, I remember spitting out my teeth. (I now have new front teeth that make for one heck of a smile). I took off my riding gloves, and while I lay there, I felt someone grab my hand. It was not an ordinary handhold, but one of confidence and purpose. I don't how much of the next few hours I was awake or unconscious. Those around said that I was more unconscious than conscious. I do remember wanting to fall asleep, and each time I tried, this hand would grip mine and keep me awake in my "un-awakeness." Looking back, I honestly believe that me trying to fall asleep was me dying and each time this hand literally kept me awake and alive.

My mom was met by a counselor and a priest, when she arrived at the hospital. She was taken into a quiet room where the extent of my injuries were explained to her in detail. They could not operate immediately on me, because they first had to wait for the swelling in my head to go down. When she was finally able to see me, she said she was able to see the white of my skull, and that there was a hole in my head. The doctors had to carry out a number of tests while we waited for the approval for surgery. No one would know the full extent of the injury, or lasting damage, until after the surgery was finished. Eventually, I went into surgery and was put into a recovery room afterward to wait. The rest was really a waiting game to try and figure out what would come next.

I woke up soon after surgery and remember that the colors of everything in the room were distorted. But I was awake and was communicating to those in the room. I told my Mom I loved her and asked who was holding my hand. I knew that it had helped me get to this point. Everyone told me that it was my head that was broken, and no one was near my hand. I knew at this moment that something bigger than me had gotten me through this close call. I didn't know it was Jesus yet but knew it was something I had never encountered before.

I had a prolonged recovery process. I had to learn how to talk normal again, walk normal again, and other life skills. Through this process, I had a mini hospital room installed at my house, and my mom would dress my wounds, etc. During this time, there was a friend from school who would come over daily and simply spend time with me. He was a Christian that come to find out was praying for me with his family that I would be healed and come to know

Jesus. His daily physical presence spoke volumes to me. He showed me Jesus when I needed Him the most. (I had the opportunity recently to go and speak at the church he and his wife planted. It was a surreal experience to come complete circle 12 years later and see how great God is!)

After a long season when I could finally leave the house on my own accord, another friend of mine invited me to church with him. My friend's actions leading up to this point gave me the confidence to accept an invitation to church. We were late arriving, and I remember walking in the back during worship. Immediately as we entered the service, I felt the same presence that I had felt holding my hand as I laid on the concrete months before. This Person that people were worshipping was the One who saved me. I was able to put a name to the person who saved my life. His Name is Jesus. I gave my life to Christ that night and watched everything change in my life.

This newfound relationship marked my life. Immediately, there was a fullness in my heart that I had never experienced. I didn't know a word from the Bible or a fancy Christian greeting, but I knew God. I wish I could say that life magically became easy, but what I can tell you is that my life now had a purpose and peace that would never leave. My relationship with God changed, and I have watched this change me ever since.

The following week at church, there was an altar call for healing. I had already responded the week before and was too embarrassed to go up front again. I found the pastor in the back after service and asked him to pray for me. After laughing at me and praying, I was healed of a lasting memory problem left over from my accident. My Mom would leave sticky notes all over the house to help remind me to do basic tasks because I simply couldn't remember. I would leave the shower on, the coffee pot on, and would even forget to brush my teeth while running out the door that I forgot to close. God healed me of this, and I watched healing take place in every area of my life. I was able to lead my Mom to a new level of relationship with the Lord and even got to baptize her on a Sunday morning. Jesus took control of every area of my life.

It is through this change that every other change is filtered through. Jesus changed the world with His life and has been continually changing my life. He wants to do the same for every person. It is only through Him that other changes can be understood because He is ultimately in control.

Your Greatest Change

Change in itself is hard enough! Without a thriving relationship with Jesus Christ, everything else is simply harder because you were not designed to do it alone. One of my favorite stories in the Bible is the story of Zacchaeus (Luke 19:1-10). Zack was living his life according to his own terms up to this point. When he encountered Jesus Christ, not only did he change, but he immediately began to change the things around him. Jesus came to him and gave him an opportunity to live life the way it was created to be lived.

> When Jesus reached the spot, he looked up and said to him, "Zacchaeus, come down immediately. I must stay at your house today." So, he came down at once and welcomed him gladly. All the people saw this and began to mutter, "He has gone to be the guest of a sinner." But Zacchaeus stood up and said to the Lord, "Look, Lord! Here and now I give half of my possessions to the poor, and if I have cheated anybody out of anything, I will pay back four times the amount." Jesus said to him, "Today salvation has come to this house, because this man, too, is a son of Abraham. For the Son of Man came to seek and to save the lost." (Luke 19:5-10, NIV)

This great shift in the life of a person is called salvation. It is what I experienced, and I believe Jesus wants everyone to experience it. Up to this point, you may find yourself in one of three categories:

1. You have never met Jesus for yourself. You may know about Him, but don't know Him. I'm not saying that you have never gone to church, people don't think you are saved, or that you do all the right actions. I am saying that you have never started a relationship with Christ.

2. You used to know Jesus, but this past season, you have begun to walk away from Him a bit. You feel like instead of growing closer to Him; you have been growing further away. Perhaps you have a secret sin or something else that is stopping you.

3. You are thriving in your relationship with Christ and you deeply desire to grow deeper with Him.

Whatever place you find yourself in the answer is the same for all of us. We simply need Jesus Christ and more of Him. We need Him to lead us and guide us into a closer relationship with Him. It is through this reality that we can move forward in our conversation about change. Regardless of where you are right now, I want us to pray this prayer, honestly together.

> "Jesus, life was meant to be lived with You. I ask right now that You would come and enter my heart in a brand-new way. Forgive me for my sins and the things that I have done that have separated me from You. Come and change me to look more like You. I want to experience salvation for myself. I ask this in Jesus' Name, amen!"

Questions for Change

1. Can you remember the first time you met Jesus? What was one of the first things He asked you to change?

2. If you needed to explain this change to another person, could you?

3. Would you describe your walk with God as growing greater each day, or growing weaker?

3

Glory to Glory

Now the Lord is the Spirit; and where the Spirit of the Lord is, there is liberty. But we all, with unveiled face, beholding as in a mirror the glory of the Lord, are being transformed into the same image from glory to glory, just as by the Spirit of the Lord.

—2 CORINTHIANS 3:17-18, NKJV

BEFORE WE START TO talk about change that happens around us, I want us to take some time to talk about change that happens inside of us. God's desire for each of us is to look more like Him to the world around us. When He thinks about us, He does so with this in mind. The world has tried to change us to look like it for our entire lives. We are in a continual state of change as individuals. The question is, who is leading the change? God or our surroundings? The world has even tried to use change to morph us in negative ways, but God desires for us to be changed and transformed according to His plan and no one else's.

Change is part of the process that God uses to truly take us from glory to glory. Notice that it is not from glory to worse. God wants continually better things for you and me, and uses change to bring us closer to Himself, and all that He has for us. If you, or I, do not believe this to be true, then we won't make it very far in this book.

Listen to the words of Zephaniah 3:17:

> For the Lord your God is living among you.
> He is a mighty savior.
> He will take delight in you with gladness.
> With his love, he will calm all your fears.
> He will rejoice over you with joyful songs.
> (NLT)

God rejoices over us, and He will use change, no matter how difficult, to change us according to His love.

Change can reveal things that most other circumstances cannot. Change causes us to question many things, and it uncovers things that were once hidden inside of us. God desires to reveal things inside of us that are not perfect. This is not to shame us, but to help us change them. God would never show something to us that He did not have a plan for helping us fix. He desires to not only show us the areas that we are weak in but also to take the next steps to help us change them.

Even if the circumstances surrounding the change are not great, God can use it to change something inside of us to become something great!

Glory

Our goal as followers of Jesus is to reflect His glory. Our growing from "glory to glory" is our growth in the ability to reflect our Creator to the world. We are changing to look more like Him. The better we are able to model and reflect Him, the more glory we can give back to Him.

Take the moon, for instance. I have always been fascinated by the moon. Different people see different things on the surface of the moon . . . I see a dinosaur. I always have, and personally, I think anyone else who sees anything different is just weird. The moon is amazing, and when it is full, you don't even need a flashlight to see outside at night. The moon by itself has no lighting abilities. Its ability to give light is only based on how well it can reflect the sun's light. If the sun did not shine its' light on it, the moon would serve no purpose. It would just be a giant floating space rock. As we grow in Christ, we must keep changing to better reflect Him to a world in desperate need of light! Otherwise, we will just be lightless rocks walking around, and no, not like the one named Dwayne Johnson.

We are not growing to reflect the sun, but the Son!

We can only be beneficial to the world and others if we reflect Christ and His glory. The world does not need a better Seth . . . they need Jesus. The more I change and look more like Him, the better for everyone. Glory is never our glory! All glory comes from, belongs to, and is always given back to God. If the Lord helps me to change, it is so that He can work better through me for the sake of others. No matter how hard the change, or how well I handle the change, the only One who gets credit at the end of the day is God.

We are being transformed into Christlikeness. This is God's desire for all of us that we would become more like Christ. Changing from "glory to glory" is something that I believe we all can continually be walking in. Changing can be the result of many different situations and can be motivated by a number of different things. God's desired end result, for all of us, is that we would be closer to Him and look more like Him in the end.

So, how do we truly change from glory to glory?

1. We need to recognize that there is freedom to change in the Spirit of the Lord

> Now the Lord is the Spirit, and where the Spirit of the
> Lord is, there is freedom.
> (2 Corinthians 3:17, NIV)

GLORY TO GLORY

There is freedom where God is. There are freedom and grace to affect the areas that we need to work on so that we can better reflect our Creator. Notice that I connected grace to changing to look more like Jesus. Sometimes, we can think that grace is something that is given so that we can continue not to change, but it is given to us also so that we can change.

> Grace enables us to change.
> Grace changes us.
> Grace establishes the relationship so that we can change.
> Grace is everything, but it never allows us to do everything.
> Grace is God giving us the ability to do the things that He has asked us to do.

> Therefore, my beloved, as you have always obeyed, not as in my presence only, but now much more in my absence, work out your own salvation with fear and trembling; for it is God who works in you both to will and to do for His good pleasure. (Philippians 2:12-13, NKJV)

It is God working in us to change; to not only want to do the things He asks of us but to also be able to do them. God has granted us the freedom to change and grow! The enemy can no longer stop us from changing, because the Spirit of the Lord is here, and where He is, there is freedom.

> Nevertheless, I tell you the truth. It is to your advantage that I go away; for if I do not go away, the Helper will not come to you; but if I depart, I will send Him to you. And when He has come, He will convict the world of sin, and of righteousness, and of judgment. (John 16:7-8, NKJV)

The Holy Spirit helps reveal the areas that He wants us to change. The Holy Spirit is different than us, in that He also gives us the tools necessary to change what He reveals. Many of us are great at pointing out issues while never having an answer on how to fix it. This is one of my biggest pet peeves, and I'm generally the one guilty of it. When an issue is identified and communicated without a suggested solution, it is called complaining. The Holy Spirit doesn't just complain to us; He helps us fix the problem. He reveals/convicts, brings the freedom needed to change, and helps empower us along the way.

If there is anyone that we want/need to look more like . . . it is certainly God!

2. We are changed through transparency and honesty

But we all, with unveiled face, beholding as in a mirror
the glory of the Lord, are being transformed . . .
(2 Corinthians 3:18a, NKJV)

I have never met anyone that enjoys being lied to. If we all were honest, we would say that we value honesty more than most things. When truth is missing from a relationship, it is very difficult to see that relationship grow, because honesty leads to trust. Trust is the building block for any relationship. I think that naturally, we are selective truth tellers and can only be wholly truthful with God's help. We, as humans, enjoy only sharing the facts that make us look better, and not sharing the things that make us look worse. If we are truly going to learn to embrace change, we need to first and continually learn to embrace being honest.

Change many times means being honest with ourselves and others about things that need to change. We think that if we share a weakness or failure with someone else, that instantly they will think worse of us. Honestly, there may be a few people that actually do, but that is not an excuse to keep it hidden. The people that want to judge you for your struggle generally have an issue of their own that they are not willing to deal with. You may even discover that when you find freedom, they are the very ones coming to you for advice and help. I've been surprised many times in my life, by other's reactions, when I have shared a struggle with someone. Rather than being judged, they generally feel free enough to open up about their own struggles and sin.

I had an issue that I kept covered for many years. I struggled with an addiction to pornography. From about the age of thirteen, up till I moved to Uganda, I struggled with this addiction in secret. It wasn't until I was finally open with people that I found freedom.

When I was 13 years old, I was visiting a friend's house while his parents were not home. He showed me a pornographic video on his dad's computer and since that day, I was hooked. Before I was saved, I couldn't tell you why it was wrong, but deep down, I knew that it was. I felt the need to hide it from my Mom and friends because it was a shameful thing. I wanted to change it, but my feeling of guilt was not enough to bring change. Once I got saved at the age of 16, the frequency of viewing pornography decreased, but never fully went away. I tried to think my way out of it, pray my way out of it, and everything in-between. I did everything except asking for help from another person. Not simply another person, but one that I respected. I knew that I wanted to change, but I had to first be honest with myself that I had a problem.

This is a big step to actually changing. Admitting to ourselves that something truly is beyond our control is hard and not easy.

I want to be extremely blunt here for a moment. Not doing a certain thing for a couple of weeks is not freedom and does not mean something is under control. Binge sinning is still sin and an addiction. Here is a great test for us in this area. Would you feel comfortable being completely honest about the area that you think is not a struggle in your life with the person you respect the most? Not about just the last week, but about the past six months? If the answer is no, or if you are looking for ways of how you would tell the story to make you look better, then you still are struggling in that area.

It is only when we are honest with ourselves that we can then be honest with others. It is then that we can ask others for help and truly start the path to change. This step is hard, but it is amazing what God can do through it! Change sometimes needs others to truly happen. That is what makes hard things so possible, and it is the way God designed them to be handled. We were created to do life together.

> I pray that right now as you read this, that there would be
> a tug in your heart. You would feel the desire to be honest

with others, and not just "feel," but truly take the step to
talk to someone. Whatever the issue is, if you have not
been honest about it to someone (preferably someone
that you respect and look up to), this is the perfect season
to do so. I promise that even though it may be difficult,
you will never regret it!

I remember the fear I had when approaching the person that I
decided to finally share this struggle with. I was convinced that I
would be met with anger and rebuke, but instead, I was met with
praise for being honest and an earnest desire to help. It was through
this conversation and the ones that followed, where I watched God
turn the page in this area of struggle. I still have temptation in this
area. This is an honest truth and why it is so vital to stay continually accountable. It is through being transparent even after extended
seasons of victory that freedom is truly possible. The only way I
have been able to stay victorious over this area has been continual
honesty.

> Confess your trespasses to one another, and pray for one
> another, that you may be healed. The effective, fervent
> prayer of a righteous man avails much. (James 5:16,
> NKJV)

I will never stop growing in purity. Even though I have dealt with
some of the big issues in this area in my life, I still have growing
to do. I have to be honest with myself continually and others, no
matter how hard it is. If I am feeling tempted in the area of purity, I
pray, talk to my wife, and call one of "my guys" that I can be honest
with. Again, this is not easy, but it is necessary.

We will talk about being accountable with change more in a
few chapters. You should have two to three people that are on your
"emergency speed dial." These are people that know you and your
struggles. They really know you, because you have let them in, and
you have given them the authority to speak into any area of your
life. Mine occasionally change depending on the season of life, but
I know I can call any one of them, at any moment, and know that
they will respond and be ready to talk.

Once a change happened in this area of my life, I began to see changes in almost every other area as well. It was as if purity was the hinge pin. Once I confronted it, eventually other changes began to happen, and those changes gave birth to other changes. Sometimes, in order for a significant change to occur, several smaller ones have to happen first.

There is a phrase that the Lord gave me during this season that I have repeated continually:

It is never wrong to do the right thing.

Changing the wrong things in our life is always the right thing. Even if the process feels wrong at times, it is always right to start. If you allow God to help you, you will continually move from glory to glory and maybe even learn to celebrate change!

3. The closer we get to Jesus, and we experience His Glory, the more we will understand our need to be transformed

> . . . being transformed into the same image from glory to glory, just as by the Spirit of the Lord. (2 Corinthians 3:18b, NKJV)

God left heaven to die on the cross for our sins so that we can have a relationship with Him, and He could restore what was lost in the Garden. In this one act of obedience, He accomplished more than can ever be written in a book. One of the biggest things He gained on the cross for us was direct access to Him. The veil that was separating us from being in direct communication with God was torn. The same Israelites who told Moses that he should talk to God for them because of their fear were now able to come before God for themselves. You and I have free direct access to the presence of God because of the cross.

The closer we draw near to Jesus, the more we are transformed into His likeness! As we experience His glory, it is like a flashlight that shows the things that do not look like Him in our own lives. It is also in His presence that we experience the peace necessary to take the bold steps towards change. I can remember so many times when I have been in the presence of God and have felt Him touching an area of my life that He wanted to work on. As difficult as it is to open those areas up, there is an overwhelming comfort in knowing that God is the one in control.

The closer we come to God, and the more we get to know Him, the more we are able to recognize the areas of our life that do not match His. Like any relationship, our relationship with God is alive. It is growing and changing. The more we learn about Him and His being, the clearer we are able to look at ourselves. Things that were okay last week are no longer so this week because we have discovered a new side of God.

It is through our constant strive for God to change us internally that we will grow in our ability to handle change externally.

Questions for change

1. What are some of the things that God is asking you to change today?

2. What are some of the things you believe need to change before you see something bigger change inside of your life?

3. Who are three people that if you needed to be brutally honest with right now, you could be?

4

The Author of Change

HAVE YOU EVER MET a friend you haven't seen in a while? Maybe they moved to a different state or started a different school, but for some reason, you have taken time without seeing them. Usually, when we see them, they seem to have changed in some way. Either they have grown taller, their hair is different, or maybe it is the way they talk. They have changed, and we notice. Some of the changes we see may be good changes, and some may be not so good. We are generally free in sharing the good changes with them. "You have lost some weight," or "You don't look like you have aged at all." The negative ones we usually keep to ourselves. What is funny, is that we have also changed, and may not even be aware.

Changes are magnified while living overseas for extended seasons. It may be multiple years that pass by before you see someone or even talk to them. It is natural to think that the next time you see a person that they will be the same as you left them. Not only that they will be the same, but that your relationship would not have changed at all either. I have found that this is rarely the case. People, circumstances, locations, shared experiences, and many other things have all changed. This doesn't always feel good, but it is a reality.

Things that once brought you together may no longer be relevant to the other party. Years ago, you may have both been into a certain sport or activity, now you still enjoy it, but they have something else that they enjoy. You can only talk about the "good ole' days" for so long. Unless you both adapt and start making new shared experiences together, it is very likely that the relationship will not make it very long. I have had many relationships that have gone both ways. Some have grown stronger and have matured as I have grown, got married, and started having kids. Others have simply died out. I wish I could keep all relationships, but I know that as changes take place, some were there to serve for a season. The best part is that it is okay! The end of something is not always a negative thing. Sometimes, it is healthy and necessary for something new to start and take place.

Sometimes, we can see change as being a bad thing. When something is different or perhaps when something does not look the way we expected, we think that it must be wrong. We even think other people should stay the same way we left them. Just because our understanding hasn't changed to match the change the person has experienced, does not mean that the person shouldn't change, or that change is bad. It means that we need to change our view of the other person to embrace the things that have changed. We need to change our view of change.

I am extremely detail-oriented, and because of this, I can generally tell when something has changed. I often annoy the people I work with because I can see minute details that I think need to change, or have been changed, and need to be put back. Most times, when I see something has changed, I want to put it back to the way it used to be. I dislike things that are different than the way I want them to be. If we were all honest, I think we would say that we are all like this in some way. I enjoy things being the same and especially being in control of when, and how, they change. This is fine if you want to live alone and isolated, but life, especially life lived with others, requires changing things even when you don't agree with the change. I have had to give up control in a lot of areas, so I don't drive myself crazy. I have had to learn to choose the battles that I think are important enough to address change.

I really like routines. My wife can testify that I could eat and wear the same things for the rest of my life. I could eat a peanut butter and jelly sandwich for breakfast every morning with a cup of coffee and be perfectly okay for eternity. I could eat pasta for dinner and wear the same type of shoes and never complain. If something works, why try to fix it? I don't need to go shopping or find something new. I have found what works for me. My wife would say that it is boring. She continually tries to get me out of my "box," and I continually strive to bring some consistency. We make a great team!

Why do we like things to remain the same?

There are many answers, but one of them is things that we can predict, and are normal, do not take any extra effort for us. They are easy because we already know the ending. We have done them before, and therefore, they are no longer new. The problem is that even if we do not want to change, everything around us is changing. If we do not change with it, we will become weird. I am no fashion expert, but I know for sure that things that were cool to wear ten years ago are no longer cool to wear today. If someone wore the same clothes every day that they wore a decade ago, people would notice. People would say that something was wrong because we were designed to continue to change and grow!

It is when we lose our ability to predict the outcome of things that cause us to rely on God for help and direction. Change gives birth to, and requires, faith on our part. Change is not the by-product of sin, but change has been tainted by sin. Change was originally created to take good things and make them even better. Sin snuck in and is trying to do the opposite. Sin tries to take good Godly things and change them to look worse and wrong.

God's view of change would be like a sunset on a clear day over the ocean. From the moment the sun starts to set, I feel like it is the perfect moment for a picture. Somehow, the more the sun sets, the more beautiful it gets. The lower the sun gets, the more the color starts to show, and it is generally right before the sun completely disappears that the sky is the most colorful. It simply keeps getting better. God desires that our relationship with Him would keep growing and changing. This agent, that God created, would be used for His glory!

The enemy desires that we would change as well. He desires that we would change for the worse, and respond to all change incorrectly. That we would see change and fear it, because of what it has done in the past, to get so stuck in a rut and become comfortable that we never grow, and never fulfill the call of God on our life. The devil tries to twist our view of change and render us ineffective, instead of making us the most effective that we can be.

God is the author of change and desires continual change and growth inside of us.

What is amazing is that He does not change, but His creation does.

> "For I am the Lord, I do not change;
> (Malachi 3:6a, NKJV)

The Lord has, and will, exist in perfection for eternity. He has never needed to change because everything about Him is perfect! All of His ways, His thoughts, and His being is as good and perfect as anything possibly could be. He is unchanging, and that is why it is so great that we get to put our trust and faith in Him. The same things He said 2,000 years ago are the same things He is saying today. He does not get moody. We do not have to feel that we need to find Him at the right point of His day after He has had His coffee, before we can ask Him something. He is the same!

I am nothing like Him in this way. There is pre-coffee Seth and post-coffee Seth. Maybe more extreme is pre-food Seth and post-food Seth. I am told that there is a drastic difference.

This is difficult for us to understand at times because we don't encounter constant things. That's what makes God so magnificent. He is nothing like anything we have found before. His love for us does not change. He literally cannot love us any more than He does right now! He loves us so much that He physically showed His love . . . Jesus.

Jesus Christ is the same yesterday, today, and forever.
(Hebrews 13:8, NKJV)

His Son Jesus, is God, and therefore, is the same. No matter the circumstance or external forces, Jesus Christ does not move or change. He lived a perfect life on earth, and while His physical body changed, He Himself did not. He did not need to. In fact, one of the biggest testimonies of His life is that He overcame one of the biggest tests . . . change. The devil tempted Him to change His mind about God. His disciples tried to change His mind about His mission. Pharisees tried to change His mind about who He was. Pain and death tried to change His obedience. No matter what, Jesus Christ overcame it all, and did not change! The fact that He didn't change means that you and I get to. I am so thankful for the ability to change!

> But whenever someone turns to the Lord, the veil is taken away. For the Lord is the Spirit, and wherever the Spirit of the Lord is, there is freedom. So all of us who have had that veil removed can see and reflect the glory of the Lord. And the Lord—who is the Spirit—makes us more and more like him as we are changed into his glorious image.
>
> (2 Corinthians 3:16-18, NLT)

You and I, on the other hand, are nothing like God, and neither is His creation. God designed us with change in mind.

God loves change, so much that He designed us and the world with change and growth at the base. He designed day to change to night. He designed winter to change to summer. He made plants to change from a seed to a tree. All of us love the story of the caterpillar transforming into a butterfly. He formed us into creatures that start as a tiny embryo, and we change constantly. All of this was a purposeful work by the author of change . . . God.

Change is a beautiful thing. While writing this book, my wife and I found out that she is pregnant. A week ago, we went to the doctor for our first ultrasound. We got to see this tiny blob on a screen. It was the most beautiful blob that I have ever seen. The little blob had a heartbeat and we both almost cried listening to

THE AUTHOR OF CHANGE

it. As thankful as I am for this beautiful blob, I am praying that it does not stay a blob, but grows and is able to serve God effectively. The whole process is incredible to watch and I find myself loving change in a brand new way. (Update: the blob has turned into literally the cutest little boy you have ever seen).

Why does God love change so much?

I believe God loves change because it proves two things to us:

1. It is an eternal proof and source of hope

Change inspires confidence inside of us, that there is always something more for us. It is not yet over and there is always an opportunity for something to change for the better. We are resting in the fact that when we eventually die, we will change from this mortal body and dwelling here on earth for heaven. This ultimate change continues to give hope to today and the difficult changes we face in the meantime.

He has put this great change in front of us for hope. Our eyes are set on heaven. Even if all the changes on earth don't make sense, we have this great change awaiting us.

> For this world is not our permanent home;
> we are looking forward to a home yet to come.
> (Hebrews 13:14, NLT)

When all other change seems discouraging, allow this great change to be encouraging. There will come a day when we will trade pain, sorrow, and sin, for an everlasting reward; eternity with Jesus. As long as we are faithful to serve Him here on earth, we will inherit heaven!

2. He loves revealing more and more of Himself to us

We get the opportunity to continually grow in our capacity to understand all that God is and has for us. The more we change to look more and more like Jesus, the more we understand who God is. Change excites God because it is an opportunity for Him to show us a new side of Himself. We can choose to see change as an opportunity to learn more about ourselves and God, or an opportunity to move further away from Him.

Change is guaranteed. It is us who decides whether we will change for the good, or if we will change for the worse. This response to all that God has for us is what will ultimately allow us to see change correctly. Change is an awesome opportunity!

I have never grown in my knowledge of God and regretted it. God is so much bigger than we can comprehend. Moses couldn't even look at God, because to even try to see all of God would have killed him. He only saw a tiny piece of the backside of God and was overwhelmed with all that God was. We get the eternal opportunity to learn more and more about the greatest being in the history of history. The more we learn, the more we change. The more we change, the more our capacity grows to learn. This will never end, and I am so thankful for that!

Growth

When God decided to create the world and us, He did so "through the eyes of growth." Everything He made, He created intentionally with growth as an ingredient. Growth and change were not some "by the way" result of creation; they are as important as anything else God created. Potential is never fully seen at the start of something. It is pretty hard to see a sunflower in a sunflower seed. You can have the best microscope, but no one can see a sunflower by simply looking at a sunflower seed. Potential is seen by looking at the end result while seeing the object being studied in its current state. If I see a sunflower and then the seed, I can see the potential even when the current state looks nothing like the end. Growth takes the potential and turns it into a reality.

Our potential is Christlikeness.

> For whom He foreknew, He also predestined to be con-
> formed to the image of His Son, that He might be the
> firstborn among many brethren.
> (Romans 8:29, NKJV)

God's ultimate purpose for us has not yet been fully seen. We can see vaguely what it is that God desires to do inside of us. Not only can we see it, but it should be our desire, to see God's desire for us come to pass. The thing that takes us from where we are now closer to our potential is growth. We should be growing every day! This is a great test for us in our walk with God. Do you look different today than you did yesterday? Can those around you see the growth in you? Are you changing and working on sin issues? Growth should not be seasonal, or annual; growth should be measured and seen daily, hourly, minutely, and secondly.

I try to have a list of things that I need to work on always at the front of my journal. It is not difficult for me to find things that I need to change or work on. When I have seen change in an area, I replace it with something else on my seemingly never-ending list of things I can grow in. I don't want to reach the end of my life thinking that I have reached perfection. I want to be growing, learning, and changing until I take my final breath. There is so much that God has for you and me! I don't want to ever have a season where I am not aware of what it is that He wants to work in me.

Questions for change

1. If you were to meet an old friend that you haven't seen in ten years, what do you think they would say is the biggest thing that has changed in you?

2. When was the last time someone told you about an area that you needed to work on?

3. If you could change three things in your life right now, what would they be?

Part 2

Responding to Change

5

Preparing to Respond to Change

THE FIRST MAJOR CHANGE in my life is one that I really do not have a lot of memory of, but it has affected a large part of my life. When I was a year and a half old, my Mom took a courageous step and removed herself and me from an abusive relationship with my biological father. It was courageous on multiple levels, but one of the biggest reasons was because it also meant removing us from all forms of normal family interaction. My Mom was born into an extreme church sect called The Molokans. They are a group that broke away from the Russian Orthodox church to pursue their own form of religion. My entire family for many generations has kept this form of church alive. You marry within the church, interact within the church, etc. The fact that she left my father meant that both of us were disowned by everyone we knew (I didn't know many people at two) and that life began to look a lot different from this point forward.

We spent the majority of my younger years moving from city to city, trying to stay away from my biological father because he had an intent to harm us physically. I have very little if any memory of the season that he was around, but the fact that I grew up without a father has changed many parts of my life. Not only the fact that he wasn't present, but that I was afraid of him had a tremendous influence on my relationships moving forward. They say a lot of issues can be traced back to "father issues," and let me tell you that I have a few! This was a change that I had no control over. Even though I had no control over it, I had to learn to live and accept it. It is a reality that I still have to choose to respond correctly to today.

Sometimes, change is not always our choice, or doing. I wish that I could say that a negative change will never happen outside of your control, but that is not true. There are many times in life that we are forcibly put in the middle of a change, and then face the choice of how to respond to it. This is a change that I have responded to in both good ways and not so good ways, depending on the season of my life. I have many times allowed external change to influence me in the wrong way. Even worse still, I have allowed negative change around me to affect how I treat others. The old adage is true, "hurting people hurt people."

Part of this change early in my life was losing a strong family connection. From two years on, it was my Mom and me, with my grandparents on occasion. It wasn't until I got saved, and was introduced to the church, that this changed. There are aspects of things that you know are hard, but aren't able to tell why until you get older and look back. I truly was in a place throughout this season where I was longing for connection. I wanted what other people had. I always felt like the odd one out surrounded by friends that looked to have the perfect family life. It is amazing when looking from the outside in how easy it is to think that others have an "easier" life than you.

Everyone has problems, and everyone has to deal with change!

They may not be the same problems as you, but everyone has things they must overcome, but as a young person, perception is everything. Everyone seemed to have parents that loved each other and siblings that were their best friends. They had huge family holidays, and people rooting them on at sporting events. I would want to spend time with them, and actively tried to force my way in to be a part of their world. Some relationships became awkward because of this, and I didn't understand the reason why in the moment. I was responding to change incorrectly, and I didn't even know. Why didn't I have what they had? Why do I feel like I am striving for acceptance? What are some of the questions you ask yourself?

As I continued to grow up, I tried to cover the reality of the effects of this change with relationships that were motivated by the wrong things. I strived to surround myself with people at all times and did whatever it took to keep people's attention and affection. I thought if enough people liked and talked to me, that the pain inside would stop. It didn't. I did not know Jesus yet and did not realize that I had a huge hole in my heart that I was attempting to fill in the wrong way. Not only was I trying to fill it incorrectly, but there was only one person who could fill it; Jesus. One change that I had no control over completely altered my path and led me to make wrong decisions along the way.

Change is something that we must learn to be aware of, and learn how to walk and process correctly. Even if we do not have complete control over it, we all have control of how we respond to it.

One of the things that makes change so hard is the fact that it is often out of our control. When we are used to something, we usually feel comfortable because we know what to expect and in return, know how to control it. If we know how someone that is common to us will respond, we are in control of how we relate to them. Familiarity is safe because we control the change. When the change leaves our realm of control, that is when it becomes scary. A new boss or person in class that we have no context for is now outside of our control. A new city or place that we have been forced to move to is a change that shakes up every piece of our life, but one of the biggest things that is affected is our level of control. If we are honest, we would admit that we are all control freaks!

Preparing to give up control

I believe a key to handling change is having an understanding of who is in control of our lives.

I spent my middle school years and the first year of high school 15 minutes from the beach in Southern California. I would spend a lot of time at the beach on weekends and really anytime I could. During my time there, I took up bodyboarding with some of my friends. It was an amazing season of fun, learning, and at times, terrifying moments. One thing I realized fairly quickly was how powerful the ocean is! Some would say that you are harnessing the power of the ocean in ocean-based sports, but really, you are just trying to hold on and make it without hurting yourself.

No matter how good you are at understanding the ocean, you can never be the one in control of it. Ship captains name all the different types of waves and currents they encounter while at sea. There is one called a "rogue wave." It is one that you can't predict, see any sign of beforehand, and it can even come in the midst of a perfectly calm ocean. It is literally a ghost in the form of a wave, that can overturn a ship. No one can say they control the ocean. You simply learn how to respond to the things the ocean does. You can't make the waves get bigger, or the water to remain calm. You do all you can to prepare, but in the end, you are at the mercy of the sea.

We need to learn from the fact that we are not the ones in control of our lives. God is. He directs, guides, and leads every aspect of our existence. Like the ocean, we may be able to judge certain aspects of what is happening, but even the greatest minds cannot predict the ocean (or anything in life) with 100% accuracy. God may choose to reveal whatever aspect He chooses about what He is doing, but the change, like the wave, can come at any moment. We are not in control of when, but once it comes, we are in control of how we respond to it.

Our response is based on how well we prepared for the change to come. If a small wave finds you unprepared, you may tumble a bit, but you will be okay. It is a different story if it is a big wave—the bigger the change, the higher the stakes. Depending on where you are, if a large enough wave hits you when you are not ready, you can break bones on a coral reef, get a nasty whiplash, and potentially drown. If you are prepared and crazy enough, there is never a wave that is too big to try to ride. I have watched videos of people riding 70' waves without a problem, and similar videos of people getting hurt with barely any movement in the water. Preparing beforehand allows you to react to the changes in the water correctly, and even though you are not in control of the ocean, you can still have a lot of fun.

Your ability to prepare for change will allow you to either respond correctly, or forever fight against something that you can't change!

Preparing for change is something that I wish I would have learned a lot sooner. After my freshman year of high school, we moved from sunny California to Central Oregon. I went from eternal summer to four distinct, and extreme seasons. The town we moved to would get over 100 degrees in the summer, and drop below zero a few days in the winter. I had only seen cowboys in movies and now I would see them in the grocery store, and sitting next to me in class. Instead of people talking about the size of waves at the beach, they were talking about the size of deer they killed over the weekend. I was not even close to being prepared for this change.

Not only was I ill-prepared for this life change, but I only had a few weeks to prepare for it. I remember thinking about how I had finally settled into some essence of familiarity in the town, and at the school I was currently attending. It felt like the moment I felt settled, was the very moment that change began to happen. This change has affected me to this day. The fact that we constantly moved made me start to feel like I had a five-year expiry date on locations and relationships. This created a fear in me that followed me for a long time. I was afraid that after this special number of years, that my relationships would change.

On the first day of my sophomore year, I walked into class with skin-tight jeans, a tight t-shirt, and long bleached blonde hair.

This was considered a normal style from where I came from in California, but not where I now found myself. To say I stuck out would be an understatement. I had forced myself to be like the culture I was previously in and was even beginning to fit it. Now, everything I had become didn't fit into the culture I was now in. Everything changed, and if I wanted to fit in, I felt like I had to change as well. I began the process of dealing with change that I could have been better prepared for earlier.

Preparing for change before it comes

I found preparing for change to be a lot like preparing to catch a wave while bodyboarding in the ocean. There is this massive body of water that people like myself try to harness to have fun. While it is true that you can become better at handling yourself in the midst of the ocean, you can never control it! It is the ocean! Unless you are Poseidon, you don't have a chance. Just like change, you have to be prepared to respond to this great force correctly.

1. Be prepared with the right equipment

One of the first things I did when I began to get into chasing waves on a boogie board was to convince my Mom to take me shopping for one. This was a task in itself, but once I convinced her, there was no stopping my love for the sport. I needed a great board, different wetsuits for different seasons, fins, wax, and a bag to hold everything. The right equipment can make a big difference when it counts, and make you look extra cool, of course. If you don't have fins, there are some waves that are beyond your reach. You have to be able to match your speed with different types of waves in order to catch them. You have to wax the "rails" of the board to add grip, or once you catch a wave, you won't be able to hold onto the board while riding. Different seasons call for different wet suits. In the summer, you may not need one, but in the winter, you need a full body suit, and maybe even a dry suit to stay warm. You may have a great board, the best wetsuit, even a good attitude, but without a certain piece of equipment, you may never accomplish what you set out to do because you are ill-prepared.

When it comes to change, there are many things that we can put in place before change takes place. Some of the biggest pieces of equipment I believe we need are flexibility, faith, and a strong devotional life.

Flexibility

When people come to visit us in Uganda on mission teams, one of the biggest things we tell them that they need to possess, while they are here, is flexibility. I'm not talking about being able to touch your toes (something I personally have a hard time doing), but the ability to respond correctly when things don't go as planned. Things, especially here in Uganda, generally don't go as planned. It is not uncommon for something to start one to two hours late, and in some cases, even the next day. When I first moved here, this was such an extreme difference from Western culture. I quickly found how inflexible I was and how I needed to change in this area. This is a tool that I am so thankful to now possess.

Without flexibility, even tiny changes can become much bigger things than they need to be. Now, I am not advocating that we become undisciplined and accept a lack of discipline in others, but I am saying that learning how not to have our world fall apart when a meeting starts ten minutes later than we planned, is a necessary skill.

The gift of flexibility is something that we can work on now to better prepare for change later. There are so many variables that we are not in control of, that to think things will always go the way we expect is silly. Here are a few questions to ask yourself to see just how flexible you are (answer yes or no):

1. When someone changes the location of a meeting (a different restaurant, or movie theater) at the last minute, it bothers you, even if you were given enough time to make the change.

2. You feel flustered when you go to your favorite coffee shop, and they have sold out of your favorite pastry. They have plenty more to choose from, except the one you wanted.

3. You are asked to share in a meeting, or at school, weeks in advance and are told you are going to share third in line. Someone is running late, and you are now asked to share second, and you now need to deal with a fit of subtle anger and frustration deep down.

4. You cannot touch your toes when you bend over (this one is a joke, and my answer is still no).

If you answered yes to any of the above scenarios, you may not be as flexible as you think. Now, I can easily get frustrated at all the above examples and sometimes do. None of them are really that important in the long run. If we are to be flexible in our pursuit of handling change correctly, we need to start with the small day-to-day things. We need to be people that can be in the midst of "nothing going according to our plan" and still be able to smile, knowing that God is in control.

Faith that God has a big plan for you

A confident, overwhelming, and not always understood faith, is the next necessary tool. Faith in God's overarching plan for our lives is so important when things change in ways that do not look like we expected. This tool has to be in place before we face a season of change. Without the foundational belief that God is in control, and that He is moving us continually closer to His plan for us and not further, we will look at change incorrectly. God is truly trying to take every one of us to a place of His goodness that we can help others also find.

We need to view change correctly in order to have full faith in what God is doing. Peter Scazzero in his book, *The Emotionally Healthy Leader* (2015), explains this correct view and the accompanying emotions in a great way:

Embracing endings in order to receive new beginnings is one of the fundamental tasks of the spiritual life — and this is especially true for Christian leaders. Not every problem can or should be solved or overcome; some things just need to be allowed to die. This isn't necessarily a failure. Often it is an indication that one chapter has ended and a new one is waiting to be written. This happens in our personal lives as well as in leadership. (Scazzero, Emotionally Healthy, Pg. 270)

He continues:

Change is difficult for most people. We experience it as an unwelcome intruder derailing our hopes and plans. We prefer to remain in control and to operate in familiar patterns, even when they fail to serve us well. We might acknowledge intellectually that God can bring new beginnings and precious gifts out of our losses, but it somehow doesn't ease the sting of loss or prevent us from trying to avoid it. It isn't easy to trust the inner voice of the Spirit inviting us to cross over into this painful and unknown new territory.

(Scazzero, Emotionally Healthy, Pg. 272)

What if change and something dying truly was a necessary step for God to take us into the next great thing? We need to view this great phenomenon of change, seasons of dying and being birthed, with eyes of faith that God is truly taking us from glory to glory. Even if the change means the loss of something, God is still in control and wants to gift us with something new.

And we know that all things work together for good to those who love God, to those who are the called according to His purpose. (Romans 8:28, NKJV)

God has a big plan for each of us. There is destiny and calling on your life. He is actively working on your behalf to bring you closer to that big dream He has prepared for you. When we allow this faith view to be the lens we see change through, we can be prepared for anything. Even if the moment sucks, the verse above helps us to believe that at some point (it may be in heaven), we will see how in that very situation, God was working for our good.

The only way that we can have this type of faith and confidence is because of the Word of God.

FAITH COMES BY THE WORD

Faith is only possible when it comes from the Word of God. In order for us to have faith in all that God is doing in the midst of change, we must have the Word of God present inside of us to grab ahold of when things are shaking.

> So then faith comes by hearing,
> and hearing by the word of God.
> (Romans 10:17, NKJV)

Without the Word inside of us, we won't have anything to anchor our emotions and thoughts to when they are tested in seasons of change. Our emotions may tell us that everything is over. Without the Bible, we may tend to believe this lie, but if we have our faith rooted in the Word, we are able to know that by faith, God is working on our behalf, even if we don't feel it at the moment.

Shortly after I was saved, I had next to zero knowledge about anything to do with Christianity. This included the Bible. Within my first few weeks of being saved, I opened up to Psalm 91. I had never heard a message on the power of the Bible, but I experienced it firsthand. I would read this Psalm every day, and no matter how terrible a day I had just passed through, this portion of scripture literally carried me through! My faith increased even though my surroundings didn't immediately change.

I believe this is the only source for true faith. People today have "faith" in so many different things. It could be the latest self-help book, the newest diet, or even a promise that was made by a person. Faith in something that is not the Bible is not true faith. All of the previously mentioned things are also prone to change. There are books written, and within a decade, the same author recants everything he said. A life-changing diet today can end in the founder dying from following the diet they started. A promise made by someone can be broken without repentance. If our faith is in those things, we will be left faithless in the end. Our faith has to be in an unshakable promise . . . the promise of the Word.

The Bible teaches that our hope is our anchor. It is something that can hold us when things are shaken.

> This hope we have as an anchor of the soul, both sure and steadfast, and which enters the Presence behind the veil (Hebrews 6:19, NKJV)

This promise comes from the Bible. Our anchor enters beyond the veil that once separated us from God and now holds to the promise, that is, Jesus. Jesus cannot be moved and does not change.

Personal Devotions

The third tool that is vital to our preparation for change is a thriving devotional life!

The constant source of all these things in my life has been my commitment to spending daily time with God. Devoting an hour every morning, for me, has been my sustenance throughout my walk with God. For us to have faith, the Word and flexibility, we need to be in a constant place of receiving from God Himself and His written Word to us. I cannot stress enough the importance of having daily time to take all the hard things in life to God and allow yourself to get to know His heart.

I can see a noticeable difference in the days when I don't start with devotions. I have less grace; smaller things bother me, I pick fights instead of avoiding them, and many other indicators. I can come to the end of a day and wonder what on earth happened, only to look back and see that it was because I failed to start my day by setting my mind on the Lord.

You could start with something small and grow from there. Maybe wake up ten minutes early tomorrow and simply seek God, and pray through the things scheduled for your day. Start by reading one verse each morning and pondering it throughout the day.

Whatever you choose to do, start tomorrow, and be faithful to do it every day. You will be amazed at what inviting God into your day will do!

These are things that we can have in place far before the season of change comes, and although it may not change the change itself, it will certainly put us on the right track to handle it correctly!

2. Learn to read the signs

After being prepared with the right tools, we need to learn how to read the signs.

There are signs you learn to look for in the ocean to decide when a good "set" is coming in. The water will behave in a certain way before bigger waves come. There are generally some small rolling waves that come before a big set comes in. Some surfers are so good at reading the water that they simply sit on the beach and wait. Once they see the right type of waves rolling in, they hop on their boards and paddle out just in time to catch the biggest set of the day. They have learned to read the signs of the water. If you learn to read these signs, you can catch bigger waves than others.

Now, there are certain signs we can look for when expecting change to come. These are not guarantees, but they can serve as things to look for as we prepare for change.

The first sign that I have seen in my own life is a general feeling of unsettledness or uneasiness. There are seasons where God begins to make things feel uncomfortable in an attempt to prepare us for change. There is the old analogy of the mommy bird making the nest intentionally uncomfortable so that the baby birds will eventually get so uncomfortable that they step out of the nest to fly.

My wife and I recently began entering into the biggest season of change for us since getting married. We began to feel a stirring inside of both of us, that was coupled with a sense of discomfort. This came at a time when things where we currently were had never been going better. Opportunities were abounding, and it seemed like the sky was the limit. The problem was that we began to feel like God was moving our hearts. There was an uneasiness that led to us both having to go to the Lord and ask Him, "Why?" As I look back, this was a precursor to change. We could not explain it at the moment, but God was beginning the process of moving us from one season to another. Any of these signs should result in us going to God and asking Him if there is something He is trying to say.

Another sign of change is the many external changes around you, that may not directly impact you, but you can see them. I have watched in my own life whenever there has been an atmosphere of change around me and involving those that I know; generally, a season of change follows in mine too. In my own immediate and extended family, there have been huge changes that have coincided with a big change for Diana and me. House sales, business sales, job changes, and many more. Amid all these external changes, we found ourselves in an atmosphere of change. It is like being in a storm and trying not to get wet. Generally, there are ripple effects of change. There may be a change of person at your work that isn't in your department, but very often, that far off change can affect where you are to some extent.

The last one I'll mention that I have seen is reawakened passion and dreams. There are seasons for different parts of life. There are things God will speak that won't be for this season, but a future one. There are times when past spoken dreams and passions begin to sit at the forefront of our minds. These may simply be for the sake of praying, but also can sometimes be a sign that God may bring a change to bring us closer to that dream.

My wife and I have lived in Uganda since we got married, and have recently heard God ask us to end our season here. Our decision to move from Uganda is a step that God is using to help bring us closer to fulfilling dreams that He has shown us in the past.

These signs are just a few that generally show up before change comes to us. These are not set in stone, and some changes occur without any warning, but I believe as we learn to expect change and prepare for it, we can become more sensitive to the signs. As much as we can be open to the signs of upcoming change, we also need to be prepared for the worst.

3. Prepare for the worst

Before getting into the ocean, hopefully, you have learned to swim and how to hold your breath. There may be situations that arise where you have to swim with all you have and hold your breath for what seems like an eternity, as you are waiting for the wave to pass. Nobody plans to be on the verge of drowning, but if you don't have an idea of what to do when things go sideways, you will often times, panic. These are things that you do not want to catch you off guard. You want to prepare for the worst and be pleasantly surprised when things go right.

Changes generally will never go one hundred percent according to plan. There are always surprises, and we need to be ready for them. We need to be secure enough in our walk with the Lord that no matter what happens, we have enough faith to know we are going to make it. We need to look at situations in front of us with our eyes wide open. We may hope for things to go a certain way, but we need to be prepared if they do not. I am not saying that we turn into pessimists where all we can see is the bad, and how everything can get worse, but we need to have a realistic expectation. A pastor once told me that no one goes through transition/change unscathed. We need to be people of faith that believe for the best but are ready if things do not go according to plan.

This also helps us make wise decisions. I enjoy riding motorcycles and going on epic motorcycle trips. I have crashed more times than I can count, and somehow my gracious wife still lets me ride. A group of guys were going on a 4-day trip to the north of Uganda and invited me to go. My current motorcycle wasn't up to the task, but one of them offered to let me use one of theirs. My wife and I sat down and said that even if I crash the bike and have to end up purchasing the motorcycle, we were ready for that scenario before I set off. We needed to be okay with a negative situation before saying yes. This is part of making wise decisions. We prepared for the worst so we wouldn't be caught off guard. The funny thing is that I ended up crashing and getting airlifted back from that trip, and we had to purchase that wrecked motorcycle.

It wasn't the best-case scenario, but we were prepared for it. (And luckily, they were gracious enough to accept monthly payments).

Our ability to not be moved by things going differently than we expected will protect us from so many of the potential danger areas of change. Discovering this tool is invaluable to us and has to be one that we continue to grow in. The next tool is what keeps us sane in the craziness of change.

4. Have tons of fun!

You may not think that fun is a tool, but it is one of the best ones we can possess. If we are not having fun, then we can get lost in all the "what ifs" and things we are surrounded with. You can prepare and ready yourself for the potential wave, but once it comes, and you are flying down the face of it, you need to enjoy it. Smile, laugh and have the time of your life.

Change means the opportunity for something new, and a chance to grow. Our faith view needs to be that God is in control, and therefore, this season I find myself in, gives me the chance to see God reveal Himself in a brand-new way. Discovering new things in other scenarios are considered adventures—the great unknown and the things that are ahead. We need to have an attitude like this about new things before the new season arises, or else, we will be starting from the wrong place.

It is change that keeps things from becoming boring and mundane. Imagine if your favorite activity never changed, and was the same thing over and over again. If you enjoyed mountain biking and rode the exact same trail every day for a year. You would eventually get bored and stop riding. You can enjoy reading more than any person on earth, but if you only read the same book over and over, eventually, you would stop. I love playing music and listening to music. I have favorite songs to play and listen to, but if I were stuck with the same one, I would come to hate it. It is change that makes things fun!

As we prepare with all these things, far before the season of change comes, we will be ready to respond correctly no matter what the situation may be. We will certainly not be perfect, and most likely will respond incorrectly and be caught off guard many times throughout our life. I am messing this up all the time! With these things in place, we have a much better chance to see change the way God does, and can, therefore, respond with faith that God is truly taking us from glory to glory!

Questions for change

1. What is one of the tools, mentioned above, that you think God is asking you to work on possessing right now? (Being prepared with the right equipment? Learning to read the signs? Preparing for the worst? Having tons of fun?)

2. What is the area of your life that you are the most afraid of changing? What is something that you can do now to prepare for a change in that area?

3. Are you having fun in the season God has you in?

6

Giving Up the Fight

CHANGE IS AMAZING IN the fact that the more it is fought against, the harder it is to manage. Change is a guaranteed thing. I had a pastor that used to tell a story about a stubborn monkey and how it led to its downfall.

The story went like this:

> There was a village in the middle of Africa that was having a problem with monkeys. The monkeys would sneak into the villagers' houses at night and steal food from their kitchens, and storage areas. No matter what they did, they could not outsmart the monkeys. They set traps and installed security lights, but it seemed like the more they did, the more monkeys came and freely took all they wanted. One day, one of the villagers came up with the idea to use the very thing they were after against them. They took a big yellow banana and placed it in a jar with a narrow opening in the top. They left the jar in the kitchen and went to sleep. In the middle of the night, they were woken up to crashing and screaming coming from the kitchen. Upon entering the kitchen, they found the monkey fighting to get its hand out of the jar. The monkey's hand was small enough to fit into the opening

of the jar, but when it closed around the banana, it was too big to remove. The monkey was so fixated on getting the banana that it would not let go. If the monkey would simply give up the banana, he would free his hand from the jar and get away. Because the monkey was not willing to give up the fight, it ended up getting captured that night.

Like I mentioned before, living so close to the beach, I learned all the different necessary components to become a good bodyboarder, like how to wear fins and get in and out of the water without falling over and looking like an idiot. You walk backward into the ocean, not forward. How to "duck dive" (getting under a wave without it taking you back to shore); how to judge if a wave was catchable or if you should just let it go, and many other ocean-related things. Before I moved away, I started to learn how to read tide reports and know when a day would be good for surfing or not. Of all these skills, one of greatest sources of knowledge came from one of my hardest lessons . . . how to crash well.

I remember one of my first times getting in the water, suited up with all my gear and paddling out. There was a hierarchy of different people in the water. The surfers had their side, and the bodyboarders had theirs too. There was a line for who was allowed to catch the next wave, and if someone had a better ride on the wave than you, you were expected to get out of their way so that they could finish. These were all things I got entirely wrong many times. After getting yelled at and spoken to by many people about all the "unwritten rules," I finally caught my first wave . . . almost by accident. I remember coming over the top of the wave and dropping down onto the face of it. It was exhilarating and scary all at the same time. I was actually doing it! The problem was that the end of the wave was coming, and I didn't know what to do next. I just held on and figured that it would somehow sort itself out. I hit the white water, and the wave crashed on top of me and pushed me far under the water. I got stuck in the "washing machine." I learned it was called that afterward. It felt like I was 100 feet under the surface, spinning and being thrashed around. I remember thinking two things: number one, I am going to die and number two, I need to find a way out of this. I tried as hard as I could to fight, and it seemed the harder I fought, the harder the ocean pushed. I was sure that Nemo and his friends were watching on in amusement as I came near-death. After swallowing a gallon of water, I eventually saw the surface and swam up, coughing up water and exhausted I made my way to the shore and sat down for a few minutes in a daze.

What just happened?

A buddy I was with came over laughing his head off and asked if I was okay. After calming down, he gave me some great advice. He explained that the best thing to do when you get caught down there is to simply relax and allow the ocean to spin you around without fighting back. Once it stops, just swim up and continue paddling back out. This seemed like such backward advice. Wouldn't doing nothing make things worse? I decided I didn't want to experience my near-death experience again, so I tried it out. I paddled back out and caught a wave. Sure enough, my problem was the same, and I got slammed down to the great deep and simply allowed the ocean to do as it wished. I was amazed at how calm and peaceful it was while being thrashed about. I didn't fight it, and in all honesty, I actually enjoyed it a bit. I felt like I had all the time in the world to think and solve the world's problems . . . much like I do every morning in the shower. Eventually, it stopped, and I swam to the surface and went back out. I learned to accept and not fight back.

Fighting against change, much like my battle with the ocean, is one of the most exhausting parts of dealing with change. This is the very thing that keeps us from moving on to the other parts of dealing with the shift that is taking part. It is not until we accept the change, and begin to process how to walk through it, will we be able to truly handle change correctly.

Let me take a moment to preface this next section by saying that there are changes we should fight against. God needs to guide us to help choose our battles and fight the ones He asks us to. God can use us to stop things from happening that never should have changed. We need to be people that walk with discernment. There may be a pillar of doctrine or belief that you hold that someone may desire to change. Those are things that we should fight for with all that we have. In this section, I'm talking about changes that are for the better or those that are incidental that may not be bad or good, but they inconvenience us in some way. These are changes that in all honesty, we have no control over . . . *the company I work for has gone bankrupt, and now I need to find another job. I was planning to go to the beach with friends this weekend, but now it is pouring down rain.* Unless you are a millionaire or Bruce Almighty, the situation is not going to be remedied by anything you can do. You need to give up the fight!

Fighting against others

In life, change is something that will always come our way, looking different each time. It can feel like it is fighting us (because it is), and our natural reaction is to fight against it. After all, aren't we in control of our lives? Who would we be if we didn't try to keep things the way we are familiar with? If we are honest with ourselves, we will admit that we enjoy the comfort that is found when things remain the same. We naturally have a hesitation towards change, and the forces that bring it. We can resent the person that brought change or the situation that arose because of a choice someone made. We can make people and scenarios the enemy simply because we blame them for the change, but more than that, because we equate them with the loss of our comfort, joy, peace, etc.

We can begin to not only fight against change but also start to fight against others. We can attach our loss of control to people, some of which are innocent, and some who are directly responsible. We then take our internal battle and turn it into an external battle. I honestly think we do this because it is a battle that we can see, and one that we feel we have direct control over. I can put a face to my hurt and fight it. The problem is this only leads to broken relationships and a longer recovery for us on the other side of change.

When I was younger, I was always told that the bigger and stronger person is the one who walks away from a fight instead of fighting. To ask someone for forgiveness even if they are the one in the wrong is the right thing to do. These are some of those things that sound easy as they are spoken, but are really hard to put into practice! If someone has lashed out at me, then I get to lash back at them. Why should I ask them for forgiveness? They are the ones in the wrong!

My wife and I are great at fighting verbally. We have a few healthy arguments each week. I have had to learn how to apologize and seek reconciliation, and how to truly forgive and move past something once I say that I have forgiven her. I am so thankful for these lessons that have been learned through the crucible of marriage. One of the things that both of us still do is justify our actions based on the other person. I argue that the reason for me being in a bad mood was because she was in a bad mood. As much as this is maybe true, it is not right. A negative reaction on my part can never be justified by someone else's negative attitude. In these instances, I have made the fight worse by fighting back with my bad attitude. I am trying to learn how not to slip into a bad mood, but to give up the fight.

In seasons of change, as everything is shaking and moving, relationships are tested. People that you have years of history with can feel like enemies, and your world can spin as mine did under the ocean. The natural response is to begin to grab hold of anything and everything trying to hold onto every relationship with as much force as necessary. We start fighting to maintain control. The harder we fight, the bigger mess we make. The truth is that there is a high likelihood of there being a loss of relationship in large seasons of change. These losses may be as simple as a shift in a relationship. The relationship may not function the same as it did before, because things that made the relationship work before no longer are the same—distance, common interests, common goals, etc. The hardest part during these seasons is when there is more than just a disagreement or shift, but a relationship actually breaks.

A few years ago, I walked through a change that cost me one of my closest relationships for a season. The other party and I were both part of the same organization. Through a series of events, my friend decided to leave the organization and pursue something else. This change shook everything I knew, largely because it was this person that introduced me to the organization that I was now giving my life to serve. I didn't handle this change correctly. I chose sides and started fighting with, and against, people. One of which was my friend. He also didn't handle the change correctly. We found ourselves on the other side of this season, deeply hurt by each other and how the other party handled the season. There were many other factors in the change, but the most painful and lasting part was the broken relationship.

It took intentionality, humility, and time on both our parts to reach reconciliation. Through many hard conversations, tears, and coming to terms with areas that needed growth, we are now able to walk in a fully restored friendship. It took a lot of apologizing and being honest about deep down motives to recreate an atmosphere of trust again. This situation didn't have to happen, and I would have done a lot of things differently. One of which would have been not to fight. I would have stayed out of the disagreements, and kept the discussions only around the things that pertained to me and the change taking place.

The only way to walk through these difficult encounters correctly is to be the bigger person and walk away from the fight. As much as it depends on you, pursue peace.

> If it is possible, as much as depends on you, live peaceably with all men.
> (Romans 12:18, NKJV)

I have found myself in many situations where it may seem justified to allow a relationship to be broken until the other person apologizes. I may feel that it is the other person that needs to come forward and pursue the mending of the relationship, because from my perspective, they broke it. Whenever I took the step to apologize for something that I felt I did wrong, the other party responded similarly. If I looked into the depths of my soul, I could always find something that I didn't handle correctly. Openness and forgiveness give room for more openness and forgiveness. Not all the relationships have been fully restored, but I have certainly changed and grown more Christlike each time.

I have made a fool of myself trying to resist change at times. I can make enemies out of people that up to this point have been nothing but good to me. I can fight for the smallest of ground, only to end up losing more than I should have in the beginning. I can slip into the age ol' temptation of only offering ultimatums. It is either this or that, when in reality, it is a mixture of both. I have to remind myself in these moments of the lesson I learned while 20,000 leagues under the sea. I need to give up the fight.

Questions for change

1. What are some current areas that you feel you are "fighting" in?

2. Can you list the relationships that are currently broken in your life, and if so, what steps are needed to pursue reconciliation?

3. What are some situations that you feel are worth fighting for, and what are some that are not?

7

When I Have to Change Too

HARD TRUTHS ARE DIFFICULT to hear. They are uncomfortable to listen to because they are true and usually mean that something needs to change. Someone once told me that the negative things we see in others are also things that we personally struggle with. It is so easy to see what is wrong in other people, but why is it so hard to see what is wrong in me?

Other people's problems have seemingly neon signs pointing to them. I bet if I asked you to look around the people you know, and list one thing that each person could grow in or change, you would not hesitate to tell me your answer. You could probably come up with a book full of ways your friends could become better human beings. I believe a big reason for this is that we love to compare ourselves to others, and in return, make ourselves feel better. It is funny when the spotlight turns on us, we shy away and try to convince ourselves and others that it is hard to find something we need to change. We are simply a step away from perfection, and people should mind their own business. Don't worry because we are also helping to keep an eye on their business for them too :)

A hard truth when it comes to change is not only that we need to change, but we are in desperate need of changing! When we stop changing, we become stagnant. Change is no longer natural and normal for us because we have stopped changing. Change outside of our control becomes more and more difficult because we stopped changing internally long ago. As we allow ourselves to be constantly growing and changing inside before the Lord, we are better prepared for the changes that occur outside of us.

Change exposes things

In seasons of change, everything shakes. It is part of how change works. Things that you didn't think were connected to the change also shake. These are times when the strength of things, including ourselves, are tested. It is in this shaking that God desires to expose things inside of us that could not have been exposed in any other way.

There was an earthquake a few years ago in a city that had been involved in a world war. After the earthquake, there was a huge crack found in the ground in the center of the city. Inside the crack was an undetonated bomb that had been there and covered up since the world war. They had to evacuate the city, and a bomb disposal squad had to come in and deal with the explosive device. For decades, people had lived their lives as normal, not knowing that just below the surface was a threat that at any moment could end their lives. It was only through an earthquake, that destroyed many things in the city, that it was finally exposed. It took the shaking to uncover a potentially deadly problem.

When I was newly saved, I heard a sermon preached on Psalms 139. The preacher talked about David and how he was not perfect, but he was always trying to change and grow. His greatest desire was to please the Lord, and he understood that God was never "done with him." One verse, in particular, stood out to me and has remained at the forefront of my prayer times. David's prayer in Psalms 139:

> Search me, O God, and know my heart; Try me, and
> know my anxieties; And see if there is any wicked way in
> me, And lead me in the way everlasting. (Psalm 139:23-
> 24; NKJV)

David had been through enough challenging moments in his life to convince many that taking a season off from changing was all right. He had every reason to simply sit back and enjoy his current season, but he never stopped pressing into God to not only change the things around him but to never stop changing him. He literally asked God to continually shake him and his surroundings and expose the deep things of his heart. Many times, God did this through seasons of change. David understood something vital: if things around him were going to change, the change needed to start with him.

I remember getting frustrated while serving as a youth pastor. I saw all the shortcomings and easily blamed everyone else, and everything else for the problems we were facing.

> If only I had better-equipped leaders on my team.

> If only we had a bigger youth budget.

> If our worship team would take more time to prepare
> and practice, surely everything would become better.

In the midst of my complaining, God reminded me of this very fact. Sure, we could grow in all of these areas, but the biggest problem was me, myself, and I. The change needed to start with me! The change I desired to see in others, I needed to first see in myself. We need to have a similar heart inside of us. May we never get tired of changing and seeking after different ways we can change to become more like our Savior. To be changed from glory to glory!

We will never stop changing if we are truly seeking after God. God's desire for us is that we would look more and more like Him. I don't know about you, but I certainly have a long way to go. The only way we can look continually more like Jesus is through constantly changing and growing. This process will not stop until it is our time to go to heaven.

Over the years, I have had many opportunities to spend time with older leaders who have had years of fruitful ministry experience and are currently still effective. I love to hear their stories and all the things they have learned over the years. They are usually full of wisdom and also have very stubborn views on things. Something that all of them have in common is the fact that they have not ceased to be in a season of learning. Some of them were born before there was television let alone a computer. Yet, you'll find them reading books, listening to podcasts, taking new courses at college, and even owning iPhones. They have made it a point to never feel like they have reached perfection, and because of this, they are amazing leaders still in their latter years of life.

Like David, old people have somewhat of a prerogative to slow their transformation pace a little, but it seems like the older they (the godly ones) get, the more they want to grow and learn!

Imagine in your lifetime seeing the first mass-produced motor vehicle, the rise and fall of Nazism and Communism. Man landing on the moon, and man descending to the deepest ocean trench. The birth of the computer, internet, and mobile phone. Travel by airplane, escalator, and the newfangled contraption called a Tesla. The discovery of Penicillin and everything that modern medicine offers. If you want to talk about a concentrated time of change, the last century was a doozy.

These elders have observed a lifetime of change, and have learned to accept and even desire it. They are my heroes, and we have a lot to learn from them when it comes to life, and most of all, change.

God desires change to be progressive in our life. He wants us to be continually aware of the things He is changing and desiring to change in us. The amazing thing about change is that sometimes, what God asks us to change is gone and dealt with forever. Other times, the change simply reaches new levels before He brings them up again to us. You may stop swearing once and for all, and there is no need to keep growing in this area . . . except when you stub your toe. Pride is something that you may reach a level of freedom in, but in the future, God may (almost guaranteed) come back and say that He wants to take you to a new level of humility.

Change is not simply something that we need to learn to cope with, but it is something that needs to become part of us! I want my name to be Seth Change Sokoloff. It would be a better middle name than I currently have! (My middle name is Harry, which was never cool until 2018 when Prince Harry got married).

One of the questions we need to ask ourselves when change is going on around us is, "God, is there anything you want to change in me through this?" If things around us are promised to change, we need to be moldable enough to change what we need to in order to remain effective. Even if the circumstance is unjustified, we still need to be open enough to allow God to use it to make us look more like Him.

God once took Jeremiah to the house of a pottery maker (Jeremiah 18). He asked him to observe the craftsman at work and then asked him a series of questions. God spoke many things, but one of the biggest was that the pot maker had the authority to not only make minor changes but to wholly destroy the pot and recreate it from scratch. That is a pretty drastic change. God will do whatever it takes to form us into usable tools for His purposes. At times, there are drastic changes that need to take place for this to happen.

I have spent close to ten years in Uganda, East Africa. I was convinced that I would die and be buried under a mango tree in the land that I love. I knew for a fact that God would never ask me to leave this place that I have poured some of the best years of my life into. My son was born here. I learned how to teach, preach, pastor, and became an elder at my church, all here in Uganda. About a year ago, the Lord began to speak to Diana and me about leaving Uganda and began to place other things on our hearts.

This urging came at a time when everything was going completely well where we were. I had more opportunities for growth in the near future than I had ever had up to this point. I had just become an elder and was asked to go and plant a new campus for our church. Surely, God wouldn't ask us to leave at this point . . .

yet, that was exactly what He was asking of us. This change would not only affect us but many people that were around us. As we began to process this change with leaders and those around us, two things were made clear. The first was that we had to be sure that God was the one calling us because not everyone was fully behind the steps that we were taking. The second was that God was going to want to use this season in-between speaking the change and actually seeing the change come to pass—to grow and transform us.

During some of these hard conversations, it was easy for me to see all the changes that others could make, how they could have handled the conversations better, and how they could have asked more questions instead of simply accusing. The issue was, while I was so clearly seeing everyone else's flaws, I was ignoring the things that God wanted to also show me. Often, what makes change so difficult is that when everything around us is changing, we blame it on the change but never on ourselves. We are not willing to change with the change. We are fine with the change benefiting us and happy to stand against change when it inconveniences us. In the midst of changes, the reality is that we also need to change.

What do we do when we need to change too?

1. We need to accept responsibility for the things that we can take responsibility for

One of the things that I had to accept in this process was that I could have handled some of the conversations better on my part. There were conversations that I could have had sooner, and I could have approached them differently. Part of the breakdown in communication I experienced in this season was my fault and something that I can change and do better next time.

There is never a season or situation that God does not want to use for His glory and to help us grow. There is nothing wasted while following God! We need to learn how to change our default when we face difficult situations. My default is to go into problem-solving mode. My wife tells me this is because I am a guy.

Generally, my way of solving the problem is blaming other people and plotting their best way forward. I need to change my default to be an inward search first. Like David, I need to ask God what it is that He can expose in me, and how to change it.

2. We need to approach the next steps with humility

A book that I think everyone should read once a year is *Humility* by Andrew Murray. I have read this book many times, and each time, God does something new inside of me. The author writes about viewing humility and the things of God through the eyes of moments:

> The life God bestows is imparted not once for all, but each moment continuously, by the unceasing operation of His mighty power. Humility, the place of entire depen-dence on God, is, from the very nature of things, the first duty and the highest virtue of the creature, and the root of every virtue. (Murray, Humility, Pg. 63-65)

It is only when we make this shift in our minds that we are able to view our changes correctly. We are to be participants in this pro-cess momentarily and seek God continuously. It is only through humility that we can view our part in situations correctly. Pride muddies the waters of change in ugly ways. This is because all we can do is think about ourselves when we allow pride into change. When we are humble enough to view the situation holistically and realize that God wants to change things inside of us, we can walk through the hardest of situations correctly.

3. We need not to walk change alone

One of the natural responses to recognizing something we need to change internally is to hide it from others. We feel that admitting something is not right is a sign of weakness. We are created to do life together and with others. It is the enemy that causes us to hide when we discover a weakness. It has been this way since the beginning. After man sinned, the Bible says that God walked into the garden and called for man. Adam and Eve, then hid behind a bush instead of freely approaching God like they had in the past. It wasn't until they revealed themselves that God made them clothes and started the process of man's redemption, culminating with Jesus on the cross.

When we recognize the areas of growth needed in our lives, we need to find others to help us walk through. Others can encourage us, give us counsel, and most importantly, hold us accountable. If I am serious about changing something, I need someone else to help me not only make a plan but to keep me accountable to actually do it. We were not created to walk change alone.

It would be so much easier if everyone else were the only ones that had to change, but we also have to change. The good news is that it is God's desire for us to grow and become more like Him. Since it is His desire, He is more than happy to help us!

Questions for change

1. What are the three areas that you want to change and grow in the next season?

2. What are some practical steps you can take to start down the path of change?

3. Who is someone that you can talk to that can help you walk through this season of change correctly?

8

My Part in Change

EACH DAY IS A new day and does not have to reflect the failures of yesterday. Your walk with God is a daily walk. Jesus told His disciples they needed to deny themselves and follow Him daily. We need to ensure that we view our walk with God this way if we are going to handle change correctly. We are going to handle situations and people wrongly as we confront change. This is guaranteed, but our response to these failings doesn't have to be set in stone!

One of the things that help us is not allowing our response to change affect the newness that God sets ahead of us. I know how easy it is in my life to respond the wrong way to change. My wrong response is never justified, and it does not have to define me or my situation looking forward. Watching my own life and responses, I can very easily allow my negative response from yesterday, to now change how I look and respond today. I failed yesterday in my attitude when met with a change, and now, as I look at my day, I see through the lens of my failure. It doesn't have to be that way. Nothing is permanent unless God says it is! Craig Groeschel addresses first steps:

It goes without saying that you can't travel back in time
and start your life over. But there is something you can
do, and you can do it today: you can start a new discipline that will make for a new and better ending to your
story. Any day you choose, you can start something new
and allow God (the finisher of your faith) to help you
complete what he called you to start. (Groeschel, Divine
Direction, Pg. 29)

We can choose today to look at the Author and Finisher of our
faith for help. He can help us take the necessary steps today that
are needed to change our response from yesterday. We can choose
to respond correctly today!

God loves to take on the task of things termed "impossible."
He waits and even longs for them. It is in impossible situations
that He smiles because He can once again prove Himself to be the
God of the impossible! One of my favorite stories in the Bible is the
story of Jesus and Lazarus. Lazarus was a person that Jesus loved
and cared about deeply. The report came that he was sick and Jesus
gave a response that doesn't make sense.

Therefore the sisters sent to Him, saying, "Lord, behold,
he whom You love is sick." When Jesus heard that, He
said, "This sickness is not unto death, but for the glory
of God, that the Son of God may be glorified through
it." Now Jesus loved Martha and her sister and Lazarus.
So, when He heard that he was sick, He stayed two more
days in the place where He was. (John 11:3-6, NKJV)

Jesus heard the report of Lazarus being sick, and He stayed where
He was. Staying, to me, seems like a lack of concern. God does
not work according to our understanding but according to His
goodness. Jesus staying actually set up one of the most miraculous
events in the Bible. According to the Jewish tradition, someone
was not fully dead until after the third day. I wonder what caused
this tradition to occur, but there must have been enough people
coming back to life during day one and two, that this tradition was
a necessity. Can you imagine going to bury Uncle John on day two,
and he pops up and asks, "What's going on?" If Jesus had come

back even one day sooner to help Lazarus, this miracle would have been less of a miracle. People would have been able to question its truth. Jesus wanted to prove the fact that He is not only the God of the seemingly impossible, but He can even bring dead things back to life! Three-day dead things!

After spending time hearing all the reasons why Lazarus being dead was final, Jesus walked to the tomb and proved to the onlookers, and us, that He truly can change any situation no matter what the circumstances say.

> Now when He had said these things, He cried with a loud voice, "Lazarus, come forth!" And he who had died came out bound hand and foot with graveclothes, and his face was wrapped with a cloth. Jesus said to them, "Loose him, and let him go."
> (John 11:42-44, NKJV)

I have seen so many seemingly permanent situations change overnight, even the ones that were because of my wrong response just a day earlier. Almost 100% of the time, it is due to my change in response and attitude. I can spend time with the Lord, shake myself up, and walk into the same situation, but with a different perspective. I force myself not to look at what defeated me yesterday as something that can never change. My response may have been wrong, but I have an opportunity today to respond differently. Jesus brought life to death, and He can surely help you and me to walk in newness today.

Our change in response can help us to deal with the change around us.

What I've written about may make it sound like I know what I'm talking about, but I want to ensure you that I am learning just as much as you. Every day is an opportunity for me to grow in something. I have more areas that I need to grow in than I don't, but this is one of the ways I ensure I am following Jesus. He is our model and example. As we compare ourselves to Him, we are met with the many areas that we "get" to grow in to become more like Him!

He calls us to change. Daily, we have this opportunity to look more like Him in everything we do. When the temptation comes to walk in failure, we need to learn how to change. We need to learn how to change our response to change. I want to talk about four ways that I have found to do this:

1. Ensure that you are okay before the Lord.
2. Identify what part you played in the situation.
3. Stir up your faith to believe for change to happen.
4. Don't allow yourself to slip into a "victim mentality."

Nothing may end up changing, and everything may remain the same, but you will be different and sometimes, that makes all the difference.

1. Ensure that you are okay before the Lord

When we fail to respond correctly to circumstances around us, we need to start by going back to Jesus. There is such a desire to run from the Lord and not closer to Him when we have fallen short in some way. Our first response must be to return to the only One that can help.

I know I can first jump into damage control mode and try to fix the circumstance that I created in natural ways. I can run everywhere trying to mend things and even slip into a cycle of trying to do good things in exchange for the wrong thing I did. None of these things help in the moment, and most of the time, I end up doing more damage and feeling more insecure, and ashamed.

Somewhere down the line, I remember that I need to start at the right place. I need to talk to Jesus about my situation as soon as possible. It is when I come before Him and begin to disassemble what I feel that I can process correctly. I ask Him for forgiveness in any area that I have sinned, and I allow Him to make a way forward for me. Often times, this entails praying for the other party (if one is involved) and for the situation at hand.

Prayer is so amazing in the way that it can change our perspective on change. Through praying, I begin to look at the same situation through a different lens. Through ensuring that my relationship with God is okay, I have a new sense of faith for whatever it is that I am going through.

My response to change is no longer what is motivating my actions. I am now motivated by God and His voice. Our right standing with God dictates everything else. This is the only place for us to start, and I have seen in my own life, is the only place that allows me to make proper decisions. It is only when I am in right standing with God that I can even apologize to others for my wrong actions.

2. Identify what part you played in the situation

I mentioned this in the last chapter, but I wanted to reiterate it in this context. We can usually identify what the other person did wrong in any context of disagreement. It is almost natural to point fingers at a person or circumstance. After talking to the Lord, we need to be honest at the part that we played in the situation, and what our attitude was. Other parties may have been the initiators or even the ones that are ultimately to blame, but 99% of the time, I know that I also had a part to play.

A wise pastor once gave me some advice in this area. He adopted what he called the "one down posture." He explained that in countless situations when he humbled himself and put himself in a place of lowliness in relationship to the other person, he was met with a positive response instead of a negative one. Even if the other party did not deserve this kind of approach, he always adopted it. It helped him get out of tickets, situations where people were asking for bribes, and most importantly, conflict with other people.

When we identify the part that we played in a situation and start a conversation with an apology and acknowledgment of what we did wrong, we set ourselves up for success. It is one thing to apologize, and an entirely different thing to apologize for a specific mistake with a humble attitude.

3. Stir up your faith to believe for change to happen

> But without faith it is impossible to please Him, for he who comes to God must believe that He is, and that He is a rewarder of those who diligently seek Him. (Hebrews 11:6, NKJV)

I can't stress this point enough other than saying we need to have faith. So often, believing that change will come is the hardest, but most necessary thing to do!

When a situation continues, and it seems like the same thing happens repeatedly, it is easy to lose faith. We can begin to see our current reality as a permanent prison cell. We need to have faith that not only will change eventually come but that God will change us in the process. Even if external change does not ever appear to come, we have changed through the waiting season and that is enough to thank God for!

Personally, I am really good at not recognizing change when it happens! I can fall into the pit of thinking that I'm not getting any better and in fact, I feel like I am moving backward. I will continue feeling this way until a situation arises where I don't react the same as I used to. Or I see an older photo of myself and think, "Wow! I have changed a lot!" Even if we don't recognize it at the moment, we are growing and moving closer to the place that God has for us! Faith is the antidote to failure. Faith forces us to believe that even if our failure looks permanent, that God is still able to use it for His glory.

4. Do not allow yourself to slip into a "victim mentality"

There is a trap that I have seen myself and many others fall into throughout the years, and that is the trap of adopting a victim mindset. It is so easy when things don't go as planned to slip into a cycle of blaming everyone else and feeling like you are the one that deserves something from others. It is very easy to behave like you are a victim of circumstance, and you want everyone to know it. While it is true that you may be the victim of an event or situation, you still have the power to choose your response.

One of my favorite examples in this area is Daniel from the Bible. If anyone had the right to behave as a victim, it was Daniel. Another nation captured he and his people and forced them to be slaves and servants of a secular king. Talk about oppression! If people didn't adhere to the cultural norms of their new home, they were killed. His friends were thrown into a furnace with the heat turned all the way up! Talk about victims! His response to the situation that he did not choose is a lesson to us in how to ensure we avoid being victims, and instead, walk as victors.

Daniel didn't understand the *why* in the moment, but he trusted that God was involved. (see Daniel 1:1-2)

Sometimes, bad things happen, and God wants to use them for our good. Daniel's situation looked pretty bad. I'm sure many of those who were around him, entered into the pits of despair. You can be an eternal optimist and struggle to see any good coming from where Daniel found himself. Imagine a foreign government coming into your hometown, and by force, leading all of you on a journey fraught with peril, just so that you could live a life of slavery. Daniel chose to trust that God was in control.

> And we know that all things work together for good to those who love God to those who are the called according to His purpose. (Romans 8:28, NKJV)

I have watched so many situations that made zero sense in the moment turn around and be used by God in my life. We have to continue to believe that God truly has the best in mind for us even if we can't see it with our natural eyes. Our response to change has to be more faith.

Daniel didn't use his situation as an excuse to sin (see Daniel 1:8).

He was a victim of captivity, yet when the opportunity came to eat defiled food, he refused. He didn't allow his situation to become an opportunity to justify sinning. The food set before the king was most likely great tasting food, but it had most likely been dedicated to idols, and Daniel knew that it was not worth sinning against God for the momentary pleasure of eating good food.

It is never right to do the wrong thing.

Daniel could have justified just about anything based on his circumstances. He could have had a bad attitude and blamed it on the fact that he was a slave. He could have lashed out in anger and fought against all who were around him and justified it because he was treated the same way, but he didn't. He chose to maintain the things God had given him. Paul states in Hebrews:

> You have not yet resisted to bloodshed, striving against sin.
> (Hebrews 12:4, NKJV)

I have not had to resist sin (yet) to the extent that the consequence was physical affliction or death. I have certainly been uncomfortable while denying myself something my flesh wants, but in all reality, it is no comparison to what Daniel faced. Yet, I have in the past, used much less as an excuse to make a wrong decision or respond wrongly to something happening around me. May we become more like Daniel!

Daniel chose to do something (see Daniel 2:18).

Instead of complaining about his situation, Daniel sought after God. God gave him ideas of how to change things around him. He sought God first for advice and not last. It is so easy to seek other sources for counsel before turning to God. When we seek other sources first, we are more likely to find justification for a wrong decision. Daniel could have found people to sympathize with him. Instead, Daniel turned to God and trusted that God would give him counsel on what to do. Daniel's decision to seek God led him to become one of the most influential people in the country. He stood for truth, and because he sought God for wisdom, he ended up gaining the trust of the king. God's wisdom is always better than human wisdom.

> But there is a God in heaven who reveals secrets
> (Daniel 2:28, NKJV).

So many times we try to figure out things on our own. God has every answer to every question we could ever ask. He has wisdom and understanding of every area of life. If we are going to respond correctly to the changes around us, we need not to simply sit around and mope. We need to ask the King of kings for wisdom and the way forward. We are not victims; we are victors because Jesus Christ has made a way for you and me!

Questions for change

1. What has been your default response when things become difficult around you?

2. What is one practical step you can take to respond correctly?

3. What is one response you can change based on Daniel's life?

9

Distraction Seems Easier

DURING THIS PAST SEASON, my wife and I have been walking through one of the biggest changes we have faced together—transitioning out of Uganda where I have spent the last ten years, and into America for a new season. I could write an entire book simply based on the emotions we have been managing. The highs and lows are unbelievable! Going from wanting to run a marathon to curling up on the couch with a gallon of ice cream. Laughing and excitement, followed by tears and heartache. Change and transition are no joke!

One thing that I have noticed in myself, throughout this season, is my tendency towards distraction. It has seemed easier to be distracted than to face the potential change at hand. Motorcycles, dreams, pizza and pretty much anything other than what is going on currently has been where my mind has led me. Thinking and placing my mind on things that are more exciting or easier has distracted me from walking through the process of this season correctly. Why is it easier to dream about riding my motorcycle around the world than it is to face what is right in front of me?

Distractions keep me from facing the reality of what I am in the midst of, and the fact that I need to face the realities of this season head-on. Avoiding change will not make it go away. Ignoring our responsibility to process the different facets of our seasons only make the reality harder to face when the change finally happens. Not dealing with change leads us to become stressed out over things that are not worthy of our stress. I have allowed myself to become anxious because I feel like I'm fighting to make something happen and I'm continually trying to avoid the obvious. We need to remind ourselves that God is in control and not us! I once again have to come back to the place of saying, "God, You can have everything and You are in charge of everything."

Distraction will keep us from being effective in our current season, and the ones ahead of us. I don't believe that we have to sacrifice effectiveness now in order to be effective later. Each season has its' own opportunity for focus and something that God wants to use us for. In order to fight distraction, we need to actively pursue certain things: seek peace in ourselves, pursue health in our relationships, and pursue edifying use of our time.

Pursue peace in ourselves

I am going to speak in general terms for a moment. Guys are terrible at acknowledging and dealing with emotions. Ladies are professional and accurate emotion recognizers and terrible emotion handlers. These over-generalizations show us one thing for sure . . . the fact that we can all grow in how we process and handle the things that go on inside of us. When I give into distraction, it is because I am failing to pursue the peace that comes from being honest with what's going on inside of me. Instead of walking through the hard path of processing emotions, I tend to ignore and simply move on from dealing with them. This can lead to skewed responses, simply because I am ignoring what's going on within myself.

My wife is great at forcing me to talk about my feelings. She can coerce honest answers from me more than just "fine" or "good." When she gets annoyed at me doing the same to her, I love to remind her of the fact that she does it to me. If I am feeling angry, even if I don't know why, I need to be honest about it. If I am feeling hurt or sad, I need to admit that I'm feeling hurt and sad. This sounds so simple, but I, for one, am terrible at it. It is only through recognizing and being honest about my emotions that I see the fruit, which is peace. The Bible says that God is looking for those who will worship Him in truth.

> God is Spirit, and those who worship Him must worship
> in spirit and truth."
> (John 4:24, NKJV)

This means that even if I am tired and weary, I can be honest with God and myself about that. True worship isn't some fake ritual that I have to be perfect for. No, when I am not feeling it, and I'm honest about that, and still choose to seek God . . . that is true worship. Peace comes from laying myself completely bare before God and those closest to me and being completely honest.

Anxiety is like your emotions breaking apart and being spread thin. As if everyone and everything, are relying on you to keep them together, but it feels like everything is just a hair out of reach. When this is present inside of us, peace is tough to find. Peace is one of two things. Either everything is literally in a place where there is no fragmentation in our life, or naturally, things are all over the place, but we have faith that God is in control of it all—like Jesus being asleep on the boat in the middle of a huge storm on the lake (Mark 4:35-41). Naturally, things looked bad, but Jesus had peace.

Distraction in hard seasons is literally us taking our focus and energy and splitting it between the pressing things in front of us, and things that aren't important. We are bringing disorientation to our minds and hearts by filling our mind and emotions with more things than necessary. Ridding distractions from our seasons of change starts with us pursuing peace within ourselves.

We need to be honest and ask ourselves what is robbing us of peace. During this past season, one of the biggest distractions for me has been looking at things online for our season in the US, looking at car options for us to buy once we get there, browsing different houses to buy and rent, etc. This may sound silly, but this has added pressure to me. Looking at all the different options, and feeling a drive to continually be aware when new things were posted, etc. Now, these are all practical things that I will need to do at the appropriate time, but now is not the right time. I was giving away energy that this current season needs to an ethereal future season. Distraction was costing me focus.

I love food. I would consider myself a food-a-holic, and if I'm dieting a "recovering food-a-holic. One of the hardest spiritual disciplines for me to be faithful in is fasting. I believe it is important for all Christians to have some form of fasting as part of their normal life and calendar. Jesus told His disciples certain things only happen with prayer and fasting (Matthew 17:21). When we think about fasting, often, we only think about food. We think about starving ourselves and how impossible it sounds. If you are like me, I would rather run ten marathons (I can't) instead of going a day without food. While a lot of fasting does mean going without food, there are also other ways to fast, and they are just as effective.

Fasting simply means depriving our carnal selves of something in order to give God the primary place in that area. If we fast food, we are saying that God is more important than my natural need for food. I think everyone should fast some sort of food when they are fasting no matter how difficult it is because our natural hunger is so powerful. We are not to be led by our stomachs, but by God. You can fast food in many different ways. It could be that you fast lunch every day for a week and take that extra hour to pray ("Man should not live by bread alone . . ."). You could cut out sugar for a month, and focus on God in a new way ("Your Word alone is sweeter than honey . . .). While food is an effective way to bring our bodies into submission, I also believe fasting other things is important.

For me, in this last season, I chose to fast looking at things to purchase. I also limited my social media intake to 12 minutes a day (my wife cut this out completely). We cut out bread, sugar, and cheese from our diet for 30 days (although we cheated one day a week on Mondays). Cutting out these distractions and bodily pleasures has helped me to focus on God in a new way. Removing some of the things that were causing my focus to spread out all over the place has allowed me to focus on this season of change. I have been able to pursue peace in myself and have enjoyed huge fruit in other areas of my life. Instead of ignoring the fact of change and giving into distraction, I have chosen to press in and allow the reality of the season to have its work in me.

Pursue health within our relationships

Another area that suffers from distractions is our relationships with others. When I am distracted with other things, I do not give the necessary attention to people. This is especially dangerous when dealing with seasons of change. Relationships are at great risk the bigger the change that takes place. When circumstances, seasons, people, and locations change, there are shifts in relationships and the things that they are made of. For me personally, this is the hardest part of change. Having to deal with other people and the changes in relational dynamics, I am tempted in these moments to give into distractions rather than work through the hard realities of relationships.

When changes occur, I almost think that an instant clean break would be easier than saying goodbye, or working through the shifts and changes that are the result of change. The truth is that it probably would be! While it may seem easier, it is not healthy, and we would regret it. Relationships take the most work, but also give us the greatest rewards! If we are going to fight the distractions in our life, we have to intentionally pursue health in our relationships.

We do this by first coming to terms with the fact that we are selfish people. We may vary in our level of selfishness, but we can all grow in becoming more selfless. I used to think that I wasn't very selfish, and then I got married. I quickly discovered that I am a very selfish person. I like things done my way, at my pace, and the way that I like them done. The problem is, in marriage and in life, it is not all about me. I may love pasta, but not everyone else does.

Pasta is my love language, just so you know. I may like to sit at a coffee shop on my day off, but my wife wants to go adventuring. I like a certain kind of paint color, and she likes the complete opposite. Neither is right or wrong, but I want my way. I have had to learn how to become more selfless. Keeping healthy relationships requires selflessness on our part.

In the midst of change, we can get so lost in everything that is happening to us that we stop caring about other people. We can retreat from others because it feels too hard. We can put false expectations on people because we feel like they should be more concerned about what we are going through, while not recognizing what they are experiencing. If we are not careful, we can allow selfishness and distractions to slip in and rob us of the very thing we need in hard seasons of change . . . relationships.

We have to be willing to have hard, honest conversations. If we are going to push through distractions, we need to be honest with other people. My wife and I are having to say goodbye to people as this season closes for us. Some of these relationships I have had for close to ten years. Everything inside of me wants to avoid them like the plague because I don't want to walk through the emotions of us leaving each time we have a conversation about it. My wisdom-filled wife explained something to me the other day that has made these conversations easier.

She explained that we have been on this journey of change for the past two years. We have had two years to process, think, and walk through the potential consequences of this change. Others are hearing about it for the first time and are starting the process at day one. Taking time to listen and process with them, helps take them further down the path that we have walked for an extended amount of time. It is extremely hard to have what feels like the same conversation over and over, but it is worth it. Instead of retreating towards distraction, I have to choose to have these conversations.

Pursue edifying use of our time

The last thing is one of the most important. We need to replace the things that distract us with things that build us. Paul writes to the Romans:

> I beseech you therefore, brethren, by the mercies of God, that you present your bodies a living sacrifice, holy, acceptable to God, which is your reasonable service. And do not be conformed to this world, but be transformed by the renewing of your mind, that you may prove what is that good and acceptable and perfect will of God.
>
> (Romans 12:1-2, NKJV)

He says that we are transformed by the renewing of our minds. The word, renewing, doesn't simply mean stopping the wrong things, but actively replacing them with the right things. I did an internship after High School, and we used to pull a lot of pranks on each other. One day, before going for a week-long retreat in the middle of summer, we put a dead fish under the seat of a guy's car in the parking lot. He was carpooling with one of us, so that meant his car would sit in the hot parking lot for a week before we got back. This was no minnow. It was a full large-mouthed bass that already wasn't fresh.

By the time we got back, his windows were fogged from the inside with one of the worst smells you could imagine. To say he was pissed off would be an understatement. He immediately removed the fish and threw it away. He then proceeded to scrub the inside of his car and even left his windows open for a week. No matter what he did, once the windows were rolled up for five minutes, there would be a return of spoiled fish smell. The problem was that he removed every ounce of the source, but hadn't yet replaced the smell with anything else. He eventually bought an entire handful of air fresheners and littered his car with them. Over time, the smell of the air fresheners, replaced the smell of the fish. The smell was so strong that he also smelled like air fresheners everywhere he went, but that was better than smelling like rotten fish.

We need to actively pursue filling our time with things that are edifying instead of distracting. I never used to enjoy reading. I was a terrible student in high school and never used to enjoy learning. As I began to grow as a leader, I had to train myself to read and to continually be in a place of learning. How did I do it? I started to read. I forced myself to get through my first book. That great feat led me to try another one. I now enjoy reading and learning, but I had to choose to force myself too. If we don't have something good to fill our time with, then distractions will become easier.

It is like the age ol' experiment. If I told you to do everything you can to not think of a giant purple giraffe, all you would do is think of a giant giraffe that looks like Barney. The only way to not think of something is to think about something else. The same is true with distractions. If video games are a distraction to you, sitting in your room thinking about how you are not going to play video games is not going to get you very far. You need to actively replace that with something else. You can decide that you are going to learn how to make fettuccini alfredo. You watch YouTube videos, practice a few recipes, and taste your labor. Why, you may ask? One day, you may want to make it for someone who is really special to you. When my wife and I were dating, I made her fettuccini alfredo for a date and I'm sure it helped my chances. Practice is really important because she became violently ill hours after eating my creation. Don't be like me and make good use of your time!

Distraction

I don't want to allow myself to become distracted from what is important in the midst of change that is difficult. I want the major things to remain major and the minor things to remain minor. It is easy for me to lend my virtue to other pursuits, that in themselves are not bad, but they distract me from what is good. Even good things that take us away from doing what we are supposed to do are not good things for us. I pray that one day, I will be so full of the Lord that even my distractions and daydreams would be of God and His coming kingdom. The bits and pieces that my mind uses to make up random thoughts would be bits and pieces of Godly things. I would be distracted by what God is doing and nothing else.

I want God to have His way in my life no matter what the personal cost is to me. I am willing to pay the price for God to be glorified in all that I do. This often means giving up certain things so that God can have more of us. Giving up things is not easy, but it is right if God asks for them. Sometimes, God asks us to give them up and they are gone forever. At times, He asks us to give them up, and after a season, He returns them to us. Other times, the second we give them up, and He sees that we are willing, He immediately returns them to us (Abraham and Isaac). God is the One in control and we need to give Him anything He asks of us.

God needs to be first in our life. I have to, more often than I like, come before God and repent for things getting out of order. Life constantly tries to take the place of God, and change can do this even quicker. If we are not careful to continue to reorder priorities inside our busy lives, we can end up putting God in the wrong place. He wants to be first, and life only works when He is! Distraction places God and the things that are important in the wrong place. Let's be people that give the best of all that we have to the most important things!

Questions for change

1. What are the top three things in your life right now that are distractions robbing you of peace?

2. What are some relationships in your life where you need to pursue peace? What is the first step?

3. What is one thing you can do to become a better user of your time? ("I will read one book in the next month . . .," etc.)

Part 3

Looking Past Change

10

Things That Never Change

THE THING ABOUT TALKING about change is the fact that we only end up talking about that . . . change. While change is a promised part of life, I believe some things in our life should never change. It is these "unchanging" things that help us with the things that always change. These things keep us rooted and firm when everything around us may seem the opposite.

Relationship with the Lord

The first thing that should never change in our life is our priority to keep and maintain our relationship with the Lord. It is when this changes that every other part of life cannot be handled the way that God would want. People handle shaking in many different ways. Some run towards the Lord more when difficulty arises, and others run further from Him. I don't know which category you fit into, but I do know which one is correct. When trials and change arise, we should find ourselves desiring to move closer to the only One that can truly help us, and that is the Lord.

I'm going to talk on both sides of this issue because I believe that our relationship with God should never change and always be changing at the same time. David, the mighty king from the Old Testament, is a great example for us in this area.

David was a person that truly experienced a large amount of change in his life. He experienced some of the most unique and trying seasons of anyone in the Bible and yet, even after failures, he maintained his relationship with the Lord. When things around him changed for many different reasons (some self-inflicted and some by others), he returned to his relationship with God. Sometimes, people around him had to push him back like Nathan, but no matter what happened, he ended up returning and focusing on the most important part of his life—his relationship with God.

Talk about seasons of life, David was a simple shepherd boy who enjoyed life tending sheep and writing songs to God. He gets grabbed from the field and anointed king without any communication on how it will happen. He slays his nation's greatest enemy (Goliath). Saul asks him to become his personal worship leader while intermittently trying to kill him. David's best friend happens to be his enemy's son. David spends years on the run hiding in caves (one of which was someone's personal toilet). David finally becomes king only to fall into sin, commit adultery, and murder an innocent man. His own son tries to take the kingdom and chases him to kill him. I could go on, but I think we can agree, David went through some changes. In the midst of a rollercoaster of a life, the Bible says that David was a man after God's heart (1 Samuel 13:14; Acts 13:22). Great change didn't ultimately change David's pursuit of a relationship with God.

We should never change the fact that this is our most important relationship. I have seen many young people start with such excitement in serving God only to see as seasons change, so does their pursuit of Him. The excuses vary for each one as does their circumstance, but the end result does not. Each one that has moved farther from the Lord finds themselves reaching a point of uncertainty and not being able to explain how they got there. When some come back, they all testify to the same thing; they wish they never allowed their life season to move away from Jesus. It is this relationship with God that brings purpose, understanding, and hope to any situation. Yet, the enemy would love to use external change to internally move us further from God.

We have to fight daily to ensure that change does not come in this area. The only way I know how to fight in this area is devoting daily time to God and His Word. I once had a pastor challenge me to give God the first and freshest moments of my day. So, my wife and I start our days with God. We both pray and read the Bible separately for a time and then come back together to discuss what the Lord is saying and pray for the day. I know for a fact that this is the reason our relationship is healthy and we have been able to endure whatever life has thrown at us this far.

God desires that our relationship with Him would never change and that we would be close to Him forever!

The other side of this is that our relationship with the Lord should always be changing, growing, and becoming fresh and new. It is easy to become stagnant and bored when it comes to our pursuit of God. It takes effort to keep it growing and changing. We need to also be seeking after a continual change towards our proximity to the Lord. We should always be moving closer and deeper in our relationship with Him.

We can never reach a place where we feel that we know everything when it comes to God. He is infinite in areas that we don't yet know. He always has something new to teach or show us. We should be continually searching and finding new ways to find Him. We cannot rely on the things of yesterday. Some basics don't change. We should seek Him in prayer, but how that prayer looks can always be changing. If yesterday you sat down while praying, why not try walking today?

Convictions

Our convictions that have been birthed in us through God and experience should also not change. Convictions are things that we feel strongly about and can back up with the Bible. These are rules that we allow to dictate decisions in our life. The greatest leaders I have known have also been those that have the strongest convictions. A circumstance would never be an excuse for them to bend their convictions. I am continually trying to be a person who lives by convictions.

I believe even stating that you have convictions in our culture today can cause others to look at you funny. People would say that nothing is set in stone and if you believe certain things, then you are worthy of a collection of adverbs: rigid, old, stale, holier-than-thou, not relevant, etc. Culture would say that everything in our lives should be moldable and changeable according to the times. The fact that my convictions don't match yours can even cause some to immediately put a barrier between us. I may not agree with your convictions, but that certainly does not make you my enemy. To be a person of conviction is not an easy thing, but I do believe it is a godly one.

The pressure to change our convictions to match those around us is real. I'm not just talking about pressure from culture; I'm also talking about pressure from fellow Christians. I have had several conversations with fellow missionaries on the subject of bribes. Living in East Africa, you don't have to go very far without finding yourself in a situation where a bribe is being asked of you. I have a conviction that paying a bribe is wrong and against what the Bible says. I have had people tell me that there are not only situations where paying a bribe was necessary but proceeded to tell me that if I don't pay the bribe, I would find myself less effective. This is from fellow Christians, and I have watched many over time change their convictions due to the pressure around them.

While others may do this, we cannot allow ourselves to fall into this trap. Our convictions are to be based on the understanding of the "ultimate truth." We believe as Christians that there is an overriding right and wrong that is based on the Bible. This doesn't change. Even if culture, surroundings, or experience change, ultimate truth does not. It is important that we do the work to ensure we know why we believe what we believe. If we are not able to prove to ourselves why we believe something, then we are simply relying on someone else's belief. We need to be certain of our convictions, and ensure that they are Bible-based, so that we can hold them in trying moments.

Your convictions on things like sex before marriage, lying, stealing, hating, and the like, do not need to shift simply because everyone around you is moving a different way. Your convictions are your convictions. Change is necessary, but not in this area!

Standards

Connected to convictions are our standards. A standard would be a rule that we may make up to keep a conviction but may not have a Biblical base. I'll give you an example of one of mine. I have a conviction that God alone is worthy of my worship, and that I should cut off any source that is contrary to God in my life. That is something that I can back up biblically, and I believe everyone should also hold this. I have a standard to help me keep this conviction. It is not something that everyone else holds, nor should they hold unless God asks this of them. I have a standard that I do not listen to secular music because I feel like it is a source of things that are contrary to God. Our standards are things that also shouldn't change simply because circumstances do. I listened to a pastor who shared a personal standard that he would not even hold hands, with the girl he was dating, until they got married. That standard sounds crazy, but he did so because he had a conviction that sex before marriage was wrong. For him, holding hands excited things that could eventually lead to breaking a conviction.

Your standards may be unique to only you, but that does not make them any less important. Your standards are what define you. People are defined not only by their standards, but how well they do or do not keep them. I adopted my standard about secular music from a pastor who discipled me when I first got saved. He believed that in all areas, but especially in the area of music, we should be cautious about what we let in and what we allow to influence us. This led him to cut off music written and sang by artists who did not glorify God. I watched him hold this standard in his life, and I believe largely because of this, he is being used by God in incredible ways.

Sometimes, we desire the anointing that is on a person, but we are not willing to make the sacrifices they have made. Some of the most influential people I know also have some of the highest standards I know. I believe they go hand-in-hand. Your ability to recognize things necessary in your life to keep you moving toward the person God desires is what will make or break you.

After adopting this standard in my life, I have seen it protect me from so many things both internally, but also externally. Knowing my personality, I know that I would have made decisions because of secular music that I would have later regretted. I am so thankful for this standard, and I know that it has helped bring me to where I am today. I have also had this standard tested many times!

I have had people mock this standard and call me "holier than thou." I have had people say that they think I am completely wrong for having this kind of standard and that I am less like Jesus because of it. Standards are not things that we can forcibly place on others and are things that we can't judge others by. We can teach others our convictions that are Bible-based, and encourage others to live similarly, but standards are personal. I can't place a standard I have on someone else, but I also can't judge another person for not holding the same standard I have.

Even if they are tested and you pay the price for them, never allow your standards to change unless God is the One who initiates it. The pastor who had a standard against hand-holding certainly doesn't have the same standard with his wife, but he still does with other women. Standards help us create boundaries that help in guarding us.

Our identity (who God made us to be)

The last area that I feel shouldn't change when everything else does is the person God made you to be. One of the most inspiring things is when someone has gone through an incredibly hard season, and they come out the other side still humble, smiling, and full of life. The person God made you to be is your precious possession. This is not something you should give away or easily change. You were created for a purpose, and this is an area you should guard against change. Test everything that comes your way and challenges you to change in this area. I believe our identity is one of the biggest things tested in seasons of change.

> Test all things; hold fast what is good. Abstain from every form of evil. (1 Thessalonians 5:21-22, NKJV)

So many young people allow themselves to change simply based on what is cool, popular, or is the most talked about on social media. You need to learn to test things before you give them influence in your life. Just because they are the loudest voice, or they have the most followers, does not mean that what they say is good. Certainly not good enough to change who you are. The only voice that should have authority to do this is God. God often uses other people, but it is our responsibility to ensure that those we give influence to are worthy of that authority. If someone is known for compromising in a certain area, or they don't have a good relationship with their spouse, I am guarded when it comes to allowing them to speak into my life. Especially in the area of making large changes to who I am. My identity is to be given to me by God, and changed by Him alone!

God Himself and His goodness!

God does not change in His love towards us, nor do His plans. One of the things that are tested in times of change is our faith in God and who He is. Remember once again:

> And we know that in all things God works for the good of those who love him, who have been called according to his purpose. (Romans 8:28, NKJV)

This truth and promise are not put on pause due to circumstance. We, in our finite thinking, tend to think in terms of "if this then that." There is even a company with this name (www.ifttt.com) that is extremely successful. It is based on a fact that if this thing takes place, then other things follow. Every time, the result is the same no matter what. God does not work this way. God works using this formula = "If God says this, then that happens." Even if the situation in normal conditions should turn out one way, and that way is not favorable to us, God can speak, and the outcome is contrary to the norm.

God is good, and He loves us!

God can work on behalf of everyone at the same time. We can't comprehend this because of our human understanding, but God works this way. We think that in order for us to work and help one person out, it means that we can't do the same for the other party involved. This is because of our limited ability, sinful nature, and many other factors. God is not bound by these things. We can be at odds with someone and God can be working towards the best for both of us at the same time. We can trust that just because it looks like someone else is moving forward, at our expense, in a season of change, it does not mean that God is not working towards our best interest.

There needs to be a conviction inside each of us that God is good. It is His nature and it cannot and will not change . . . ever!

> For I know the plans I have for you," says the Lord. "They are plans for good and not for disaster, to give you a future and a hope. (Jeremiah 29:11, NLT)

We may not be able to fully see exactly what God is doing now, or what He desires to do in the future, but we do not need the whole picture in order to believe that it is bright. No matter where you find yourself today while reading this book, God has great things in store for you if you would choose to trust Him. The decisions you have made up to this point, and the consequences that have followed, may paint a picture of an impossible situation. Here is the truth to believe: God is the only thing that is beyond the realm of change. Everything else (no matter how permanent it looks) can change, and be used for God's glory.

Joseph understood and believed this:

> You intended to harm me, but God intended it for good to accomplish what is now being done, the saving of many lives. (Genesis 50:20, NIV)

His situation and life had more changes then most! He went from the safety of his father's home, to being sold as a slave, to incurring death threats, to rising to leadership, and everything in between. He was tested in his belief of God's goodness. Although on the outside it looked like God was not working towards good in his life, he chose to believe that God was.

You may not feel that things are changing for the better currently, but choose, like Joseph, to trust God and His goodness.

Questions for change

1. Can you clearly list your standards, and convictions, and explain why you believe them?

2. In the last season, what have you felt the most pressure to change that you know you shouldn't change?

3. Even if they look impossible, what are some ways your current situation could turn around, or turn out for good?

11

Moving Forward Towards Fruit

REGARDLESS OF EVERY FACTOR of change, God desires that we find ourselves moving forward after change and not in any other direction.

Sometimes, change leaves us with an uncertainty of what is ahead of us. We can leave a familiar season and enter a season of unknown. Times like this can be scary. How do you take steps forward if you can't see where you are going? In a natural sense, walking in the dark is hard. I generally have to go to the bathroom a couple of times a night while sleeping. When I was single it didn't matter how much noise I made when I got up, because I was the only one in my house. Now that I am married, I try as hard as I can, not to make any noise when I get up. No matter how hard I try, I simply do not have night vision. My feet always find the corner of the nightstand, or dresser. I open the bathroom door too hard, or trip on something on the floor. It is naturally difficult to maneuver in the dark, and it is the same spiritually. This is one of the biggest tests for us in the area of change. We are forced to walk by faith and not by sight.

Your word is a lamp to my feet and a light to my path.
(Psalm 119:105, NKJV)

In ancient Bible days, before the creation of flashlights, people would wear small lanterns mounted to their feet. Imagine trudging around the dessert in highly flammable clothing with a tiny fire strapped to your sandal. I am enough of a klutz to surely trip and light myself on fire. I would bring a whole new meaning to being the "light of the world." The light was only enough to show them where to step next. It didn't shine far off in the distance; it only gave enough light so that they could safely take one more step.

The Word of God and His dealings with us is just like this. He knows at times that if we could see the whole picture, we would certainly try to make it happen on our terms. It takes faith for us to step out when the only thing we can see is the next step. When it comes to change, we wish we could see how the entire change would end up. We want to know how everything will settle. Sometimes, all we can see is a tiny pebble in front of us, and that can be scary. The place we have just come from is familiar to us, and there is always a temptation to turn back. Listen to Paul's summary of the great fathers of our faith:

> Obviously people who say such things are looking forward to a country they can call their own. If they had longed for the country they came from, they could have gone back. But they were looking for a better place, a heavenly homeland. That is why God is not ashamed to be called their God, for he has prepared a city for them. (Hebrews 11:14-16, NLT)

The fact that they never looked back made God so proud that He was not ashamed to be called their God. What did God tell Lot's wife? Don't look back! Everything God has for us is in front of us. He desires that we would have our eyes and faith so fixed on what He has ahead for us, that when change happens, we do all we can to find ourselves moving forward.

The fruit of change may be a season that looks worse than the season you just left. An opportunity may not have been as good as you thought, or perhaps, it now requires more work than you had originally planned. There is a temptation to want to return to the season you just left and live in a place of comfort. Behind can look brighter than what is ahead, and what is currently surrounding you. Surely, the season before the change took place is better than the current season, and what can it hurt to go back to a place that we have come from?

I remember after about a year of living in Uganda, I became really homesick. I started to miss friends and the ease of life in America compared to that of Uganda. I allowed myself to become preoccupied with my past and lose focus on where I was. I started to entertain "what if" thoughts. What if I was in the US and not here? I would have this and that, etc. It was during this time of focusing on a past season that I noticed even my dreams began to change. Instead of dreaming about the opportunities in front of me, I was dreaming about things that would take me back. I started giving more time to a non-existent reality than to what I was actually doing. I was daydreaming about the wrong things. I had lost focus.

During this time, I received an email and eventually a phone call from a church back in the US. They were offering me a dream job (at that time) back in a setting that I was used to. Great pay; a comfortable living situation until I found my own place, and a step back to where everything was familiar. To say that I was tempted would be an understatement. Suddenly, I had a chance to change my current path. I could justify a decision to move back to America. I could easily say that God could use me anywhere, and to say anything different would be wrong. I could convince everybody else, but there was a problem. Was this a change that God wanted?

Part of faith is allowing ourselves to believe that what is ahead with the Lord is always better than where He has brought us from. Even if our current season does not look, feel, or even smell better than where He brought us from, God desires to continually move us forward towards the things He has for us. Faith is required in every part of life, but especially when walking in seasons and through changes when we cannot fully see the other side. Looking back is not an option that you and I have!

If I were to move and take this opportunity, I would not be anywhere near where I am today. I'm sure God would have used it and I would still be loving people and serving Him, but I would not be where I am today. It would have been the wrong decision at the time. I would not have met Diana, and although doing good, I would not be fulling the will of God for my life. I know this because I have full confidence that where I am today is exactly where God desires me to be, and even through there are changes directly in front of me, I am moving closer to what God has for me.

The Danger of Familiarity

We may never fully give in to the temptation to return to where God picked us from, but we can do something just as dangerous; we can give in to the temptation of familiarity. There is nothing wrong with familiar things. I love things that I know and have experienced. Familiarity becomes dangerous when we allow it to begin to dictate our decisions. We can begin to make where we currently are to look like where we came from. Instead of asking God what He would have us do, we can start to make changes based on what is familiar. This is the complete opposite of innovation and Godly creativity, which are incredibly valuable in seasons of change.

When given the opportunity to make a change, we can fall back on what we know. We can begin to make statements such as:

"We used to . . ."

"Back in the ol' days . . ."

"Before the change . . ."

"The old leader used to . . ."

Now, it is never a bad thing to make decisions based on the experience God has given us. In fact, the best decisions made are those that are made through the lens of past experience, and those that have gone before us. We learn from past mistakes, so we don't make the same ones. We are all building off the people who came before us. The error is when we default to these things without seeking God for our decisions. We can begin to make changes in our life to make our current place in life look more familiar, and even look like where God brought us from.

Many preachers have made the statement, "It took only one day for Israel to get out of Egypt, but forty years for Egypt to get out of Israel." God was calling Israel forward, but even though their physical location changed, they still were stuck in the past. They longed for familiarity. God needed to work inside them, to break the cycle of wanting what they had known in the past. What was familiar to them was continually leading them to sin, and backward instead of forward. When Moses spent a long time on the mountain with God (Exodus 32), the Israelites decided to make a god like they had seen in Egypt. They literally started to recreate Egypt in the new place that God had brought them! If we are not careful, familiarity will kill us.

God desires to use us to create positive change to take His purposes forward. When things are changing, or we are given the opportunity to be part of a change, there are two questions to ask ourselves. First, "Is my response based on my past and what is familiar, or is it based on what God is saying for now?" Second, "What new thing does God want to do through this change?" There are incredible ideas sitting inside each one of us. God wants to do a new thing in and through us!

Throughout history, the greatest ideas and innovations came in response to problems. People realized the things that currently existed were not the solution to the problem they were facing. Instead of doing what they had seen before, and what they were familiar with, they created something brand new. I wonder how many people have silenced the opportunity to be innovative be-cause of the temptation of familiarity? I know I certainly have at times. I have many times responded negatively to change, and slipped back into old habits instead of allowing God to use the season for something new.

May we be people that take the faith step to seek God for new ideas and answers to the problems we face. If we do so, we have a better chance of receiving the fruit of change.

The fruit of change:

Change, in the end, ends with things changing:

> Change can lead to change in relationships with others.
> Change can lead to a season of ease.
> Change can lead to a season of difficulty.
> Change can lead to bigger and bigger change.
> Change generally results in more change!

You may or may not know the magnitude or scope of all the things that will ultimately change. Change affects you and those around you. Walking through seasons of change, I am shocked at areas that I never thought would be touched by a simple change, are sometimes the biggest areas to change. I think of the story of the "butterfly effect." Whether this is true or simply science fiction, I do not know. It states that if you were to go back in time and simply change the flapping of a single butterfly's wing, that the end result would be enormous. The butterfly would not have flapped at the right time to add the smallest gust of wind to push the tiniest speck of dust into motion to affect something else. The end result being some horrific hurricane, or something because of a mis-flap of a butterfly's wing. It sounds pretty out there to me, but I think it is an interesting picture of the power of change.

Change can lead to a change of direction for you and others.

God can have you on a set course for a season, but after a time, He may ask you to change direction. These are hard changes that will likely cause change in others as well. This result is genuine and should always be on our minds when we process change. Being honest about the effects of change can lead to not making a change, or changing with our eyes wide open to the possible result, or even allowing God to work a new idea through us in the process.

The great potential fruits of change are the possibilities God has placed ahead of us. When God brought the Israelites out of Israel and changed their surroundings, the purpose was to take them to the "Promised Land." On their journey, they sent spies to see if the land was truly as great as they had heard. One of the greatest things they decided to bring back to show their fellow countrymen was fruit:

> When they reached the Valley of Eshkol, they cut off a branch bearing a single cluster of grapes. Two of them carried it on a pole between them, along with some pomegranates and figs. (Numbers 13:23, NIV)

One of the fruits of their season of change was literally "fruit." Not just fruit, but fruit so big that a cluster of grapes had to be carried by two people! Change may be hard, painful, and incredibly uncomfortable during the process, but there is fruit on the other side of it: greater endurance, stronger character, and the opportunity for a greater relationship with the Lord. The fruit is so much better than the familiarity of the past. It won't look anything like where God brought us from—it will appear a million times better!

They say a journey starts by taking the first step. For the Israelites, it was stepping into the Red Sea. For Peter, it was stepping out of the boat. For me, it is moving from a place that I have called home for the last ten years. Your next step may be terrifying in every way, but you have the opportunity to make it a step forward and not backward. Just think of the fruit that is waiting for you.

Questions for change

1. What are some areas that you feel tempted to "go back" to?
2. What are three brand new ideas that you feel could help you in your current season solve a problem?
3. What does "taking a step forward" mean for you?

12

The Waiting Game =
an Opportunity for Hope!

OUR FAITH FOR CHANGE is that it will truly be used to take us from glory to glory. Our faith is rooted in hope. All change can be viewed with hope if we have faith to believe that God is truly working towards better things for us. I don't know where I would be without hope. Hope that even in the worst circumstances, God is still sovereign and in control—He has been my lifeline. The problem is that hope isn't really hope unless we are in a place where we need it. One of the most difficult places to be is in the middle— waiting. The middle of change is one of the hardest places!

I have heard since I was young, "Patience is a virtue." While I know in my "knower" that this is true, I still struggle with patience. One of the hardest things for me to be patient about is waiting for something that I know is sure to happen, to actually happen. After Diana agreed to be my wife, there was a period of waiting between asking her, and us actually getting married. It was a sure deal that we were getting married. The date was set, the plans had been made, the dress bought, but there was still a stretch of time before we would be husband and wife. I had a hard time being patient. People that have multiple year-long engagements have a grace that I do not! This was to be one of the biggest and greatest changes in my entire life, but I had to wait for it.

It is in the middle of these change seasons that God prepares us for upcoming seasons of bigger change. In this case, I was aware of the season and the upcoming change, but this is not always the case with transitions in life. Sometimes, we are in seasons that seem to be change free, but we need to be aware of where we are. We need the Lord to help us understand the season we are currently living in. Perhaps we don't know exactly what the change that is coming will look like, but He can help us to prepare now with eyes of hope. In fact, Jesus wants us to learn how to understand the seasons we are in.

> He replied, "You know the saying, 'Red sky at night means fair weather tomorrow; red sky in the morning means foul weather all day.' You know how to interpret the weather signs in the sky, but you don't know how to interpret the signs of the times! (Matthew 16:2-3, NLT)

As we look past change and grow in our understanding of change, we need to learn how to read the signs so we know where God has us. It is in the in-between seasons of change that God works on us internally to prepare us for the next season. I needed to learn patience in-between getting engaged and getting married so that I could be a better husband. Diana can testify that I am still growing in this area, but I have grown by leaps and bounds. I would not have had the opportunity to grow in patience, had it not been for this season of waiting.

The time of waiting is truly when our character is shown, when hope and our faith is put to the test. Can the change that we are sensing come to fruition while we remain faithful in the in-between moments? It is in the waiting that we have the opportunity to understand hope in a brand-new way. Listen to what Paul says to the Romans:

> Therefore, having been justified by faith, we have peace with God through our Lord Jesus Christ, through whom

also we have access by faith into this grace in which we stand, and rejoice in hope of the glory of God. And not only that, but we also glory in tribulations, knowing that tribulation produces perseverance; and perseverance, character; and character, hope. Now hope does not disappoint, because the love of God has been poured out in our hearts by the Holy Spirit who was given to us. For when we were still without strength, in due time Christ died for the ungodly. For scarcely for a righteous man will one die; yet perhaps for a good man someone would even dare to die. But God demonstrates His own love toward us, in that while we were still sinners, Christ died for us. (Romans 5:1-8, NKJV)

Our faith is rooted in Jesus Christ. Faith is impossible without Him because faith in anything else is false. Only faith in Jesus is true faith because He never fails. This faith grants us access to grace, which is hope! We have hope because Jesus granted us access to God through His death, burial, and resurrection. His obedience secured us access to a relationship that allows us to walk in full confidence of the One in whom we trust. Jesus came to die for us and literally gain hope for us! He is our hope and the foundation of change in our lives.

Romans gives us a model for how we can receive this unwavering hope. Tribulations lead to perseverance, and perseverance creates character, and character gives birth to hope.

Tribulations

Paul said we are to "glory in tribulations." Hope is birthed in hard times. I don't know about you, but my first response to something difficult is not joy. If I were to be honest, my first response is generally frustration, anger, a bad attitude, and pretty much anything other than joy. The Bible says that we are to glory in these hard things because we know what they will produce. This is only possible if we have faith in Jesus Christ. This becomes possible when we allow ourselves to view hard seasons here on earth as opportunities for us to meet Jesus in a brand-new way. It is in the hard, middle moments that we get to see a brand-new side of Christ that we would not have seen in any other way. Hope has a name, and it is Jesus Christ!

Jesus never promised a lack of trials but assured us that in the midst of the trial, He would be there with us. He promised that in the midst of the storm, He would be in the boat with us, helping us hold on for dear life. I think Jesus smiles when storms come because they give us the opportunity to see a brand-new side of Jesus. You can't call Jesus your healer unless you have been sick, and He has healed you. You can't call Him provider unless you have been in need, and He has provided. You can't call Him father to the fatherless unless you have been in a season without a father. You can't call Him the God and Lord of change unless you walk through change with Him. We need to look at tribulations with joy and hope, saying, "I wonder who I get to meet Jesus as this time?"

The Israelites would give the Lord new Names based on the things He revealed to them. They had some of the most unique names for God: He is our "banner;" He is our "rock;" and He is our "shelter." These are names that you don't just think of off the top of your head. These are names that are only possible if you have walked with God through something and He has shown Himself to you in a brand-new light. Yes, God is our "friend," but when you are friendless and you meet Him, this name means something completely different.

Hope means that I can look at the hardest parts of change, that are beyond my understanding, and ask, "Jesus, who are You to me today?"—because my hope has a Name.

Perseverance and Patience

Paul said that difficulties give way to perseverance, and my constant growth area, patience. It is through viewing and navigating shaky times correctly that perseverance is created in us. We are able to grow and overcome something bigger the next time around and are equipped for even bigger changes. James, the brother of

Jesus, certainly experienced his fair share of change and struggles. He writes in full faith:

> My brethren, count it all joy when you fall into various trials, knowing that the testing of your faith produces patience. (James 1:2-3, NKJV)

He learned from personal experience that if we can make it through the immediate emotions, and everything that surrounds difficult seasons, there is another side. There is a purpose and life after even the hardest of changes.

I would not consider myself to be in great shape, but I have had plenty of seasons when I try to workout regularly. If you have ever been to the gym, you understand what it means to lift weights. You don't find the lightest ones and use them to become stronger. You find the ones that are almost too heavy for you. You struggle lifting those for a season, and eventually, the weights that were too heavy now become manageable. You then move onto something heavier and so on. I rarely reach the "so on" stage, because I struggle with being consistent at my gym visits, but I understand the principle. In order to carry something "heavier," you need to lift something "heavy." As the "heavy" increases, the "heavier" will also increase. The goal of trials is perseverance. The ability to face something bigger, scarier, harder, and not give up, but instead, keep going because you understand that with God, you are able.

I have joy in hope because I can now look at the same situation, or thing, that defeated me last time and know that I can now overcome. I have seen worse and overcome before, so I can certainly handle whatever is in front of me. The purpose of trials is to work perseverance in us and greater hope in all that God can do! I have seen God heal before, so there is no reason He shouldn't heal this time. God didn't fail me last time, why would He this time? I now have confidence in Him and in what He is doing inside of me, and that gives me hope!

Character

Paul then goes on to say that if we persevere, there is something greater than simply "making it." We grow in our character. Our ability to handle ourselves correctly in seasons of change will either mark our character positively or negatively. Character says that not only have I been through a hard thing and persevered, but I have come out the other side with experience, and I am able to tell other people how to overcome the same. I now own my response, and my character has been proven not just by words, but by action. I have allowed change to have its work in me, and I now look more like Jesus. I've grown from glory to glory.

It is when we have proven what we believe with our character that we receive the confidence that we are seeking—confidence that only comes from hope!

Hope

Hope is what carries us through the constant barrage of change that awaits us. Our hope is founded in an unshakeable fact that is far beyond what we can see or imagine. Even if the worst of the worst happens and we die (I don't know of a more intense change than ceasing to exist on earth, and beginning to exist in eternity), we have the hope of our salvation! Listen to Peter proclaim this truth:

> In this you greatly rejoice, though now for a little while, if need be, you have been grieved by various trials, that the genuineness of your faith, being much more precious than gold that perishes, though it is tested by fire, may be found to praise, honor, and glory at the revelation of Jesus Christ, whom having not seen you love. Though now you do not see Him, yet believing, you rejoice with joy inexpressible and full of glory, receiving the end of your faith—the salvation of your souls. (1 Peter 1:6-9, NKJV)

The end of our faith, and all the different things that happen in our lives, ultimately is the saving of our souls. Our focus is on eternity and all that God has for us. This is where we are going to end our conversation about change because it is the most important. We must have hope that can look past whatever the picture is that our current season of change is painting. The only reason that I have hope that I will be a good father, after growing up without one, is because I know that God is changing me to look more like Him. He is the greatest Father anyone could ever ask for. Without change and the hope of change, I would have zero chance at being even close to a good father.

Change truly does have the ability to take us from glory to glory. Changes we didn't ask for. Changes that leave us hurt and in pain. Changes that we have to work for. Changes that we have to wait for. Changes that cost us everything we have. Changes will stretch us, challenge us, and ultimately change us. I know with full confidence, that if we allow God to be the focus of change, He will use them to take us further in His purposes. He will use them to take *you* further in His purposes! I know this because I have hope. Hope that we all are being changed into the image of God through change!

> But whenever someone turns to the Lord, the veil is taken away. For the Lord is the Spirit, and wherever the Spirit of the Lord is, there is freedom. So all of us who have had that veil removed can see and reflect the glory of the Lord. And the Lord—who is the Spirit—makes us more and more like him as we are changed into his glorious image. (2 Corinthians 3:16-18, NLT)

Questions for change

1. When was the last time you had to wait for something, and what was your response to the waiting?

2. What is a tribulation that you are currently enduring, and what character trait can God work in you through it?

3. Do you feel like you have hope for change, and why?

Bibliography

Groeschel, Craig. *Divine Direction: 7 Decisions That Will Change Your Life* (p. 29).

Scazzero, Peter. *The Emotionally Healthy Leader: How Transforming Your Inner Life Will Deeply Transform Your Church, Team, and the World*. Zondervan. Kindle Edition.

Murray, Andrew. *Humility* (Optimized for Kindle) (Kindle Locations 63–65). Kindle Edition.

The New King James Version. Nashville: Thomas Nelson, 1982. Print.

Tyndale House Publishers. *Holy Bible: New Living Translation*. Carol Stream, IL: Tyndale House Publishers, 2013. Print.

The New International Version. Grand Rapids, MI: Zondervan, 2011. Print.